FOREIGN STUDENTS AND INTERNATIONAL STUDY

Bibliography and Analysis, 1984-1988

Philip G. Altbach
Jing Wang

UNIVERSITY
PRESS OF
AMERICA

nham • New York • London

National Association for
Foreign Student Affairs
In Cooperation with the Comparative Education Center
State University of New York at Buffalo

Copyright © 1989 by

National Association for Foreign Student Affairs

University Press of America,® Inc.

4720 Boston Way
Lanham, MD 20706

3 Henrietta Street
London WC2E 8LU England

Printed in the United States of America

British Cataloging in Publication Information Available

Co–published by arrangement with the National Association
for Foreign Student Affairs

Library of Congress Cataloging-in-Publication Data

Altbach, Philip G.
Foreign students and international study : bibliography and analysis,
1984–1988 / Philip G. Altbach and Jing Wang.
p.   cm.
Rev. ed. of: Research on foreign students and international study. 1985.
Bibliography: p.
1. Educational exchanges– –Bibliography. 2. Foreign study– –Bibliography.
3. Students, Foreign– –Bibliography. I. Wang, Jing. II. Altbach, Philip G.
Research on foreign students and international study. III. Title.
Z5814.E23A43   1989   89–2852 CIP
[LB2375]
016.37019'6– –dc19
ISBN 0–8191–7371–1.
ISBN 0–8191–7372–X (pbk.)

All University Press of America books are produced on acid-free paper.
The paper used in this publication meets the minimum requirements of American
National Standard for Information Sciences—Permanence of Paper for Printed Library
Materials, ANSI Z39.48–1984.   ∞

Contents

FOREWORD

With the publication of *Foreign Students and International Study: Bibliography and Analysis, 1984-88,* the National Association for Foreign Student Affairs continues its special association with the Comparative Education Center of the State University of New York at Buffalo in publishing timely bibliographies and policy commentary on topics related to international study and foreign students.

Philip Altbach, with his SUNY-Buffalo colleagues, has emerged in recent years as the principal bibliographer of the literature on international student mobility. He is bringing important comparative views to his bibliographies by the inclusion of publications on educational exchanges that reflect the research and policy focus of countries other than the United States. Japan, the European Community, and Australia have in recent years formulated ambitious national policies to attract foreign students and/or to expand study by their students abroad. Competition for foreign students among the "economic summit" countries is increasing—each nation seeing in educational exchanges strong national interests and opportunities to enhance global competence and intellectual influence. Emerging economic and political interests are stimulating more policy attention to international education. At the same time, there may be a shifting of attention away from the traditional scholarly and cultural objectives in exchange.

Altbach and Wang have suggested in their introductory essay a set of research "challenges." NAFSA looks forward to working with international education colleagues in facing these challenges and specifically to working with Altbach and the Comparative Education Center in future collaborations.

JOHN F. REICHARD
Executive Vice President
National Association for
Foreign Student Affairs

Acknowledgements

This volume was made possible by a grant from the National Association for Foreign Student Affairs and with the support of the Comparative Education Center, Faculty of Educational Studies, State University of New York at Buffalo. The volume stems from a long-standing interest in issues relating to foreign students and international study. Earlier work was supported by the Exxon Education Foundation, NAFSA and the Institute of International Education and resulted in several publications. These publications include:

Philip G. Altbach, David H. Kelly and Y. G-M. Lulat, *Research on Foreign Students and International Study: An Overview and Bibliography* (New York: Praeger, 1985)

Y. G-M. Lulat and Philip G. Altbach, *Governmental and Institutional Policies on Foreign Students: Analysis, Evaluation and Bibliography* (Buffalo, NY: Comparative Education Center, SUNY at Buffalo, 1986)

Elinor G. Barber, Philip G. Altbach and Robert G. Myers, editors, *Bridges to Knowledge: Foreign Students in Comparative Perspective* (Chicago: University of Chicago Press, 1984)

Philip G. Altbach, "The Foreign Student Dilemma" *Bulletin of the International Bureau of Education*, No. 236-237 (1985), pp. 7-92.

Philip G. Altbach and David H. Kelly, *International Development and the Foreign Student: A Select Bibliography* (Washington, DC: National Association for Foreign Student Affairs, 1984)

We are indebted to Pat Glinski and Nancy Myers, who composed this publication.

PHILIP G. ALTBACH
JING WANG

Buffalo, New York
July 1988

Introduction

This volume is divided into two parts -- a short essay discussing current trends in the literature on foreign students and international exchanges and a select and annotated bibliography on this topic. The bibliography consists of 519 items, the majority of which are annotated. The bibliography is divided into 31 sections to guide the user. This bibliography is an update of *Research on Foreign Students and International Study: An Overview and Bibliography,* published in 1985. That volume included 2,811 listings covering materials published up to 1984. This publication includes items published between 1984 and early 1988. It is organized according to similar categories in the 1985 publication. We selected the most valuable items for annotation and in our annotations tried to provide a basic understanding of the item as well as to indicate the key findings. Of course, it is impossible to include more than a preliminary summary in a one-paragraph annotation.

This bibliography is selective in that we have chosen items deemed to be relevant to a broad understanding of foreign students. We have included books, doctoral dissertations and theses, articles and magazine reports and, to a lesser extent, reports and government documents. We have not included unpublished material because such items are usually difficult or impossible to obtain. Our rule of thumb was to include material that can be obtained in a good library or on a readily available data base. Within each subject category we have listed materials alphabetically, with books (and theses) first and articles second. In a few instances, we have included key items of reportage along with the articles but we have not systematically listed shorter articles from magazines and newspapers that relate to our topic.

This bibliography is international in scope. We have included items from a number of countries. While the large majority of our listings are in English, we have included items in Japanese, French, German, Russian and Spanish as well. English dominates the literature on foreign students -- the key publications are in English and the largest number of the world's foreign students are studying in English-speaking countries.

The publication updates our earlier 1985 volume. It also follows the pioneering effort of Seth Spaulding and Michael Flack in their

INTRODUCTION

The World's Students in the United States: A Review and Evaluation of Research on Foreign Students, published in 1976. Our efforts are different in that we are concerned with presenting as comprehensive an overview as possible of the field, while Spaulding and Flack were largely interested in providing an analysis of the research.

The organization and conception of this bibliography is straightforward. We hope to serve those concerned with foreign students and international study by providing as comprehensive a bibliography as possible of material published since 1984. We feel that those concerned with policy as well as academic officers and researchers concerned with foreign student affairs will find this publication useful. We are particularly interested that policymakers in Third World nations, the major "senders" of foreign students, be aware of the currents in the literature and the key research available. It is hoped that this bibliography will provide a useful resource base to help inform policy, practice and research concerning foreign students and international study.

Foreign Students and International Study: Research and Development

Philip G. Altbach

An earlier bibliographical volume, *Research on Foreign Students and International Study An Overview and Bibliography*, published in 1985, included 2,811 items covering a twenty-year period up to 1984.[1] The bulk of the listings in that volume were recent. Since that publication, the literature has grown even more rapidly, and that growth is reflected in the fact that this publication, covering only a five year period, includes more than five hundred items. This brief essay will focus on some of the broad trends in the literature that are reflected in this bibliography and indicate some of the areas in which further research and analysis may be useful. One of the problems with the research on foreign students and international study is that it is not in the mainstream of any field. It is unusual for a sociologist or political scientist to take up, on his or her own initiative, research on foreign students. In the field of educational studies, there has been some interest in foreign students by scholars in comparative education -- indeed, a number of the key surveys of the field have been by comparative educators.[2] The fields of guidance and counseling and educational psychology have also contributed to the literature. Both of these areas have contributed significantly to the training of professionals in the field of foreign student affairs, and research has been a by-product of these training programs.

It is, in a way, surprising that an enterprise that involves about one million students worldwide, which spends significant amounts of money and which deals with important issues of knowledge transfer and international educational relations has generated only a modest research literature. When seen in its full context, foreign students and international study is an important, complex and significant phenomenon. Too often, however, the field is seen through the lens of one of its segments, such as the economic impact of foreign study or issues relating to English language training. As a result, the full implications of foreign study are not evident.

While a significant segment of the literature focuses on policy issues relating to foreign study, there is little evidence that policymakers take this analysis seriously.[3] Policy issues relating to foreign students are evident at the level of individual academic institutions in the host countries which must provide needed services for foreign students and must organize international study efforts. Governments are also faced with policy issues. Sending countries must weigh the implications of foreign study -- economic, political, curricular, etc. -- and there is very little research to help guide decisions. Host nations have a better knowledge base on which to make decisions concerning such issues as "full cost" for foreign students, possible restrictions on entry and other matters, but again it is not clear that the available research is actually used by policymakers.

The literature on foreign students remains dominated by a few countries, although it has become significantly more international in recent years. The concerns of the major host countries, especially the United States, the United Kingdom, Canada and Australia, dominate the literature. It is likely that at least 75% emanates from these four countries. The literature is largely in the English language. Recently, there has been an increasing amount of material in German, Japanese and to some extent French as well. There is also a Russian language literature, reflecting the more than 65,000 foreign students studying in the Soviet Union, but this literature is not generally available outside the USSR. The research and publication on foreign students and international study done in the Third World -- source of most of the world's foreign students -- is miniscule. It is surprising that these countries, which have such a major stake in foreign study, have taken so little interest in generating data and analysis relating to the issues from their perspective.

Despite limitations and lapses, the literature on foreign students has expanded dramatically. That growth seems to be continuing. It is useful to identify the major sources of expansion.

Sources of Growth

A traditional source of research on foreign students is doctoral dissertations done in several fields, most notably counseling psychology, psychology and English As a Second Language. Foreign students have constituted a source of data for studies of individual psychological adjustment, language issues and related questions. The number of such dissertations seems to have remained relatively steady over the years. This genre of research is both less prominent a part of the literature now because of the growth of other sources and because many of the studies tend to be repetitive of earlier work and therefore not pioneering work. A majority of the dissertations seem to be in these few areas, although dissertation research is slowly expanding to other areas, including educational policy, the economics of foreign study and a few others.

Sponsored research concerning foreign study is a new but highly important and influential phenomenon. Most of the key work on foreign students stems from sponsored research. It is noteworthy that the funds expended for such research and publication in the past decade have been extremely modest, yet have resulted in some impressive work. Several agencies have been responsible for the bulk of the sponsored research on foreign study. These are:

in the United States, the National Association for Foreign Student Affairs (NAFSA) and the Institute of International Education (IIE);

in Britain, the Overseas Students Trust and the United Kingdom Council for Overseas Students Affairs (UKCOSA);

in Canada, the Canadian Bureau for International Education; and

in the German Federal Republic, the Deutsche Akademische Austauschdienst (DAAD)

In addition, the publications series of the American Association of Collegiate Registrars and Admissions Officers (AACRAO) concerning higher education systems and credential evaluation in a number of countries is also very valuable. Each of these organizations has its own particular interests and orientations. NAFSA, for example, has been particularly concerned in its work to provide material valuable to practitioners in the field. It has also, through its Education for International Development program, sponsored research dealing with specific issues of foreign students from Third World nations. NAFSA has the largest publications program in the field, reflecting its large membership and range of interests. The Institute of International Education has for many years published its *Open Doors* volumes, which provide the best overall statistical summary of the situation of foreign study in the United States. IIE has recently sponsored research on a variety of topics relating to foreign student policy, and these are especially relevant.[4] The Canadian Bureau for International Education has been concerned with policy issues relating to foreign study in Canada and with compiling statistical material relating to foreign students in Canada. Because overseas students have been the focus of a national debate in Britain for most of the '80s, there has been a considerable amount of research and publication, some of it focusing on key economic issues. Both UKCOSA and the Overseas Students Trust have been active in publishing material. The trust has also sponsored several key studies.[5] The DAAD in West Germany has long been concerned with adjustment issues relating to foreign students in Germany as well as with policy related and statistical material. In Japan, the Research Institute on Higher Education at Hiroshima University has focused some attention on foreign students and foreign study issues as Japan attempts to internationalize its higher education system and rapidly increase the numbers of foreign students in Japanese universities.[6]

There have been a number of official commissions dealing with aspects of foreign study and international study in countries such as Australia, Canada and Japan. In the United States, the President's Commission on Foreign Language and International Studies provided data and information. These reports typically collect statistical and other information, and their documents are a valuable source of insights.

These are among the factors that have contributed to the impressive and seemingly sustained growth in the literature on foreign students and international study. The growth has been in part haphazard, depending on the predilections of graduate students and the various crises that occur from time to time. It has also, for the first time, been partly directed by the concerns of the major organizations which deal with foreign study. Conscious efforts have been made to identify key research needs and especially to develop analysis that relates to major policy issues, such as the "full fee" debate in Britain. To a very limited extent so far, government agencies (notably the Agency for International Development and in West Germany the DAAD) have invested small amounts of funds in research and dissemination efforts. A few private foundations (such as the Mellon Foundation, which has provided funds for IIE research efforts) have also been convinced that foreign study is a topic of importance.

If a field which is on the verge of "takeoff" is to be sustained and to continue the impressive work that has been started in the past decade, those concerned with both research and with policy relating to foreign study -- organizations like NAFSA, IIE, the Council on International Educational Exchange and others must ensure that the impetus that has been started is continued, that there be some coordination of effort, that the funds available for research and dissemination be expanded, and that the research and analysis that emerges receive the attention that it deserves. Efforts must also be made to ensure that research on foreign study move into the mainstream of concern of the scholarly disciplines, particularly the various subfields of educational studies, psychology, economics and sociology. A topic like foreign study is inevitably interdisciplinary, and this is both a plus and a minus. It is an advantage in that it can involve researchers from a variety of fields in pathbreaking work. It is a minus because there are few established methodologies, and many scholars are reluctant to stray far from the confines of their disciplines. Sustaining growth and more effectively targeting key topics for research and analysis remains a challenge. But much progress has been made, and it is imperative to sustain the initiative.

Recent Trends

It is very difficult to generalize about a large and diffuse field of study, but several broader currents seem to be evident based on the material reported in the 1985 bibliography and on the items in this bibliography.

There is a steady flow of doctoral dissertations relating to foreign students and international study -- most of which deal with microstudies of specific groups of students, specific institutions and the like. Most dissertations use psychology as the base discipline or are concerned with English As a Second Language. The overall quality of these dissertations varies considerably. It is my impression that while the dissertation literature was at one time the most important single element of research and included some pathbreaking research, this is no longer the case.

There continues to be an almost total domination of the literature by the industrialized nations. Virtually all studies are published in the industrialized nations and reflect the concerns and debates in these countries. The lack of analysis of issues effecting the major "sending" nations, such as the economic costs to the sending countries, problems of absorbing foreign trained professionals and the like, is a serious matter.

Statistical information is increasingly available and accurate. While UNESCO has been somewhat less active in collecting and publishing statistics, national agencies have been more involved. The European Community has been increasingly involved with data collection concerning foreign study, and this will further strengthen the data base. Information concerning Third World nations remains the most difficult to obtain, and data relating to the European socialist countries is also spotty. Overall, however, there is fairly good information concerning statistical trends, flows of students and the like.

There is an increasing amount of literature relating to policy concerning foreign study. This trend is, of course, related to the important policy debates that have taken place especially in

Britain and Australia, but also an awareness in other countries that the policies implemented by governments and by academic institutions relating to foreign students have an immediate and widespread impact. There is an understanding in the research community that policy is an important topic, but there is so far only limited evidence that the research and analysis is used by those responsible for policymaking.

Challenges

Based on this bibliography, it is possible to identify areas which need further research as well as some possible new approaches. This final section is intended to posit a tentative research agenda for the coming period. The topics suggested here, if added to the already strong inventory of research, will significantly strengthen the field.

Third World perspectives. The lack of material by Third World researchers concerning specific Third World nations and relating to broader Third World policy concerns is startling. There needs to be a better balance in the research and analysis. Of course, the major responsibility for identifying topics and developing research agendas and strategies rests with Third World researchers and agencies, but a broader consciousness of the problem and the possibility of providing multilateral funding may also be advisable. International agencies such as UNESCO might play a role, and organizations like the International Development Research Center (IDRC) of Canada, which has a strong tradition of sponsoring joint research projects, might also be helpful.

Curricular issues. Curricular policy issues have not received much attention in the literature. Foreign students may find that the curricula that they study overseas are not relevant to their needs. There is need for consideration of how the academic curriculum of the industrialized nations might be adapted to better meet the needs of foreign students. It is probably impractical and perhaps even unwise to significantly alter established domestic curricular practices, but much can be done through special workshops, etc. to relate the curriculum to foreign student needs and concerns.

The Microeconomics of Foreign Study. The economic literature relating to foreign study is quite new -- and so far rather limited. The research that exists is largely concerned with broader economic policy issues. There is a need to be better understand the economic impact of specific foreign student populations on academic institutions and the individual economic circumstances of foreign students. In general, economic issues need much more attention.

Comparative Studies. The vast majority of the research relates to foreign student issues in one country. This is not surprising because much of the literature is concerned with specific national issues or "small scale" doctoral research. A comparative approach could yield some useful insights. The experience of other countries may be useful in understanding specific issues, and comparative studies would provide broader perspectives.

Minority Groups among Foreign Students. The most important and currently rapidly growing foreign student minority group is women. Female foreign students have received scant attention in the literature. They have special problems, concerns, reentry problems and the like. Refugee students have received little attention in the literature, and are an important group as well. Without question, the research on foreign students has tended to see the foreign student community in aggregate, differentiated only by nationality. The lens needs to be focused much more clearly on specific populations within the foreign student population.

Privately Funded Students. It is possible that a majority of the world's foreign students are privately funded -- by themselves or their families. Privately funded students need research attention. Their attitudes, values, economic and other problems all need attention. The issue of whether privately funded students tend to remain abroad more frequently than sponsored students after their studies also needs further consideration.

Foreign Students from Industrialized Nations. It is likely that as the European Community implements its ERASMUS program, which will open the EC's borders for academic pursuits and as a greater international consciousness takes hold in American higher education, the numbers of students from industrialized nations studying outside their borders will increase significantly. Yet there is very little research on the motivations for study abroad, problems such as language and adjustment, economic issues involved and the like.

The Impact on Academic Institutions. To date, research has related to individual students or broader policy issues. Yet the impact of foreign students on the academic institutions hosting them is considerable in terms of the use of resources, social factors on campus and the like. More attention needs to be paid to the ramifications for academic institutions of foreign student flows.

The Foreign Student "Industry." The network of organizations and services that deal with foreign students is impressive. Organizations like NAFSA are a major force in the field. Academic institutions offer training for professionals. Programs for foreign language training (especially in English but also in other "metropolitan" languages) are extensive. A series of sub-professions now relate to foreign students. There has been considerable debate over recruiting foreign students. Recruiters are part of an emerging "industry." Yet there is virtually no research on this topic.

Foreign Scholars. There is a large group of people who are not enrolled for degree programs and who do not come abroad under the various "student visa" categories. These individuals are lumped into a category frequently referred to as "foreign scholars." They number in the many thousands. Yet there is virtually no research concerning this important group of individuals.

The list could go on, but based on the available literature and this author's perspective of research needs, this seems to be a useful compilation of topics deserving attention. Translating a list of concerns into a workable research agenda is, of course, a complex task. To some extent, the network already exists. There is a group of organizations in the major industrialized nations that has been concerned with foreign study issues. This network could be mobilized to consider a detailed research agenda and obtain funding. There is an urgent need to involve Third World countries as well. Perhaps UNESCO, which has faced severe problems in recent years but which now has new leadership, might be able to help. An international consciousness is needed. A commitment to bring research findings to the attention of appropriate policymakers both in government and in academic institutions is required. Additional funding for research and dissemination is an essential ingredient, but the amounts of money required need not be very large.

Foreign study and international education are key issues in postsecondary education worldwide. Perspectives differ, of course, from country to country. The problems faced by the major "sending" countries are different from those in the "host" countries. With more than a million students studying outside the borders of their own countries, with Western Europe about to embark on one of the most extensive programs of encouraging foreign study ever undertaken, with Japan seeking to drastically increase its numbers of foreign students and with debates concerning funding, curriculum and other impacts taking place, foreign study has become a major concern worldwide. It is time that the more attention be given to the provision of relevant research and analysis and to the dissemination of this material.

Notes

1. Philip G. Altbach, David H. Kelly and Y. G. M. Lulat, *Research on Foreign Students and International Study: An Overview and Bibliography* (New York: Praeger, 1985).

2. See, for example, Elinor G. Barber, Philip G. Altbach and Robert G. Myers, eds., *Bridges to Knowledge: Foreign Students in Comparative Perspective* (Chicago: University of Chicago Press, 1984).

3. For a policy-related bibliography, see Y. G. M. Lulat , P. G. Altbach and D. Kelly, *Governmental and Institutional Policies on Foreign Student Analysis, Evaluation and Bibliography* (Buffalo, NY: Comparative Education Center, State University of New York at Buffalo, in Cooperation with the National Association for Foreign Student Affairs, 1986).

4. Craufurd D. Goodwin and Michael Nacht, *Absence of Decision: Foreign Students in American Colleges and Universities* (New York: Institute of International Education, 1983) and Lewis C. Solmon and Betty J. Young, *The Foreign Student Factor: Impact on American Higher Education* (New York: Institute of International Education, 1987), among others.

5. Peter Williams, ed., *The Overseas Student Question: Studies for a Policy* (London: Heinemann, 1981).

6. J. Hicks, "The Situation of Asian Foreign Students in Japan," in *Higher Education Expansion in Asia* (Hiroshima: Research Institute on Higher Education, 1985). pp. 141-155.

Guide to the Use of the Bibliography

This bibliography is organized according to thirty-one categories. While we have tried to make these categories as clear as possible, there is inevitable overlap in coverage. The following listing provides a brief definition of each category and an indication, where relevant, of other related categories for cross-reference usage. It is hoped that readers will look under the relevant topics for related materials.

Definitions for Categories and Guide to Cross References Searches

1. *Reference and Bibliographic Materials.* Includes bibliographies, foreign student handbooks, and guides for students from abroad.

2. *General.* Includes general theoretical discussions of the foreign student issue and broad works on foreign students in several countries or from several countries or broad geographical areas (Asia, Europe, etc.). See also "Specific National Studies," and "Statistical Materials."

3. *Statistical Materials.* Includes statistical compilations and analysis on foreign students in general. Also see "Specific National Studies."

4. *Historical Studies.* Includes items with mainly historical emphasis, including the recent (since 1950) time period if from a historical perspective. The items here are relevant as background to other topics in the bibliography.

5. *Policy of "Sending" Countries.* Includes work on national policy and philosophy for sending students abroad, both how and why they should travel. See also "Economic Aspects: Cost-Benefit Analyses of 'Sending' Countries" and "Overseas Study and Socioeconomic Development."

6. *Policy of "Host" Countries.* Includes work on national policy and philosophy for receiving foreign students. See also "Economic Aspects: Cost-Benefit Analyses of 'Host' Countries."

7. *Economic Aspects: Cost-Benefit Analysis of "Sending" Countries.* Includes work on broad economic consequences of sending students abroad both from national and personal perspectives. See also "Overseas Study and Socioeconomic Development," and the next category.

8. *Economic Aspects: Cost-Benefit Analysis of "Host" Countries.* Includes work on the broad economic consequences of receiving foreign students.

9. *Overseas Study and Socioeconomic Development.* Attempts to isolate work linking foreign study to the development process. See also "Attitudinal and Behavioral Studies," and "Curricula and Programs of Study."

10. *Legal Issues.* Attempts to isolate the technical problems of national policy and cross-cultural contact.

11. *Recruitment: Policies and Procedures.* Includes works on programs and abuses of recruitment. See also "Reference," "Evaluation of Credentials," and "Language Related Issues."

12. *Admissions: Policies and Procedures.* Includes works on the admissions process and standards. Also see "Reference," "Evaluation of Credentials," and "Language Related Issues."

13. *Evaluation of Credentials and Equivalence of Degrees.* Contains works which describe the content of specific nations' educational systems and general discussions of making degrees more uniform. Also see "Admissions: Policies and Procedures."

14. *Finances: Sources and Problems.* Focuses on how students are able to pay for their education. Also see, more broadly, the economics section.

15. *Health.* Includes work on the health problems of studying in a new environment.

16. *Counseling Services.* Includes work on all forms of counseling -- personal and academic. Also see "Adaptation Problems."

17. *Adaptation Problems.* Includes many studies of the student fitting into a new environment. Also see "Attitudinal and Behavioral Studies," "Specific National Studies," and the next category.

18. *Academic Performance.* Assessment of why students do well or poorly academically. Also see "Evaluation of Credentials," "Adaptation Problems," and "Language-Related Issues."

19. *The Foreign Teaching Assistant.* Includes broad discussions on the foreign teaching assistant problem and how their teaching can be made more effective. Also see "Language-Related Issues."

20. *Attitudinal and Behavioral Studies.* Attempts to present the broad psychological work on foreign students. Also see "Adaptation Problems" and "Academic Performance."

21. *Cross-Cultural Issues and Activities.* Includes broad works on international exchanges and their philosophy.

22. *Curricular Issues and Programs of Study.* Includes broad study of curricula and the debate on their relevance for foreign students. Also see "Disciplinary Studies."

23. *Language-Related Issues.* Attempts to include the material that deals with language training, testing, and other problems. Also see "Admissions," and "Academic Performance."

24. *International Educational Exchange and Study Abroad.* Attempts to isolate the material on specific study-abroad programs and specific international exchanges primarily at the graduate and post-graduate levels.

25. *Disciplinary Studies (Engineering, Agriculture, etc.).* Includes the curricular and special problems of specific types of disciplines for foreign students when the focus of the work is on the area of study.

26. *Specific National Studies.* Includes work that focuses on a single nationality group studying abroad and foreign students from several countries studying in one country. Also see "General" and "Attitudinal and Behavioral Studies."

27. *Specific Institutional Studies.* Deals with foreign students at a specific institution, hence focuses on student problems of those particular institutions.

28. *Women International Students.* Includes work where women are the primary focus. Also see "Academic Performance," "Adaptation Problems," and "Attitudinal and Behavioral Studies."

29. *Return and Reentry Issues.* Includes work on fitting foreign trained personnel into both the social and economic life of their home countries. Also see "Overseas Study and Socioeconomic Development."

30. *Alumni.* Work on how institutions of higher education have attempted programs for foreign alumni and how foreign alumni perceive the impact of their foreign study. Also see "Return and Reentry Issues," and "Overseas Study and Socioeconomic Development."

31. *Foreign Student Advisers and Personnel.* Includes work on the professionalization of a growing academic staff area.

1. Reference and Bibliographic Materials

Books

Altbach, P. G. and Kelly, D. H. *Education for International Development: International Development and the Foreign Student: A Select Bibliography.* Washington, D.C.: National Association for Foreign Student Affairs, 1984. 18 p.

A bibliography of approximately 160 items dealing specifically with issues relating to international development and foreign students. The listings are not annotated. Among the topic areas are reentry issues, curriculum and international development, the brain drain and attitudes relating to development questions.

Altbach, Philip G.; Kelly, David, and Lulat, Y. G. M. *Research on Foreign Students and International Study: An Overview and Bibliography.* New York, NY: Praeger, 1985. 403 p.

A major bibliography, partly annotated, of 2,811 items covering the period between 1965 and 1984 relating to all aspects of foreign students. This 403-page volume is divided into 37 chapters relating to various aspects of foreign students and international study. The volume begins with a 65-page analytical essay which discusses the trends in the literature on foreign students and broader currents in the development of policy relating to foreign students and international study.

Bachmann, P. *Auslandsstudium und Ausländerstudium in der Bundesrepublik Deutschland. Eine Bibliographie (DAAD Dokumentationen und Materialien 4) (Foreign Study and Foreign Students in the Federal Republic of Germany: A Bibliography).* Bonn: Deutscher Akademischer Austauschdienst, 1984.

Barnes, Gregory A. *The American University: A World Guide.* Philadelphia, PA: ISI Press, 1984.

A guide to American higher education, aimed mainly at foreign students and scholars. The organization of studies and of the university, among other topics, are considered.

Berry, Stan. *Entering Higher Education in the United States: A Guide for Student from Other Countries*, revised edition. New York, NY: College Entrance Examination Board, 1985. 53 p.

This volume presents advice for foreign students about postsecondary education in the United States and an overview of U. S. education. Steps that should be taken before applying for admission include using existing information, selecting programs and institutions, and requesting materials from selected institutions. One resource is the Foreign Student Information Clearinghouse, and a list of clearinghouse processing centers in 20 countries is included. Also provided is information on the application process, records of previous education, English proficiency tests, academic entrance examinations, financial aid forms, obtaining visas, and orientation programs.

Bibliography of Available Literature Relating to the Recognition of Studies, Diplomas, and Degrees and to International Mobility in Higher Education. Bucharest, Romania: UNESCO, European Center for Higher Education, 1985. 120 p.

Bibliography on Foreign Student Recruitment. Washington, D.C.: NLC Foreign Student Recruitment Information Clearinghouse, 1985.

Breustedt, Ch. *Das Auslandsstudium im Spiegel Neuerer Literatur*. (Foreign Study in the Light of Recent Literature). Hannover: Hochschul-Informations-System, 1984.

Connotillo, Barbara Cahn and Johnson, Christine, eds. *Specialized Study Options U.S.A. A Guide to Short-term Programs for Foreign Nationals*. New York, NY: Institute of International Education, 1984.

Describes the short-term programs, from technical courses for beginners to executive development programs for professionals, that are accessible to or specially designed for foreign nationals. For each of the 875 such programs representing 17 major and 46 minor fields of study, information is provided on sponsor's name, program title, subjects and unique program features, beginning or ending dates or duration of sessions and the registration period, location of instruction, methods of instruction, eligibility, cost, availability of scholarships, type of housing offered, application deadlines, contact persons, program numbers, and program highlights. Also provided is information on U. S. service organizations that provide housing, study programs, counseling, information services and publications.

Danckwortt, D. *Auslandsstudium Als Gegenstand der Forschung -- eine Literatur Übersicht (Werkstattberichte 11) (Foreign Study As the Object of Research: A Literature Survey).* Kassel: Wissenschaftliches Zentrum für Berufs -- und Hochschulforschung an der Gesamthochschule Kasssel, 1984.

An annotated bibliography of 54 books and reports, mostly in German, relating to foreign student and international study, this publication provides an overview of some of the more substantive literature relating to the topic in the German language. The items were written between 1960 and 1984.

Directory of Overseas Education Advising Centers. Washington, D.C.: College Entrance Examination Board, 1985. 80 p.

Ebel, A. and Mohr, B., eds. *Higher Education in the European Community. Student Handbook* (4th edition). Brussels/Luxembourg: Commission of the European Communities, 1985.

A concise guidebook, prepared by the European Commission, concerning postsecondary courses and programs in the countries of the European Community (Belgium, Denmark, the German Federal Republic, Greece, France, Ireland, Italy, Luxembourg, the Netherlands, and the United Kingdom). Listings of institutions, specific programs of study, admissions requirements, language required, etc. are provided. There are also data on the organization of academic programs.

Financial Planning for Study in the United States. A Guide for Students from Other Countries, revised edition. New York, NY: College Entrance Examination Board, 1985.

A guide for foreign students who need information on the cost of higher education in the United States, this volume addresses the responsibilities of foreign students in meeting these costs, the types of financial help that may be available to them from colleges and other sources, and how to apply for financial aid and to plan the financial aspects of their stay in this country. It particularly focuses on tuition and fees, different kinds of university and non-university housing, and awards from U. S. government services, aid from the IIE and from six agencies serving particular nationality groups, college aid to undergraduate and graduate students, and financial aid from sources outside the U.S.

Other subjects discussed include problems of currency restrictions, transfer of funds and using U. S. banking services, travel, books and supplies, medical and dental services, health insurance, clothing, expenses for married students and their dependents, and orientation and English language programs, the addresses of education credit agencies in 14 Latin American countries are also provided.

Friendship with an International Student: A Guide for New American Host Families. Washington, D.C.: National Association for Foreign Student Affairs, 1984. 7 p.

The guide offers advice for American families who host foreign students, with attention to culture shock, the first visit, stages of the student's adjustment and mealtimes. It suggests that both the host and foreign student can learn from the other. Also, a frank discussion of differing conceptions of friendship may be helpful for both the student and the host. The foreign student advisor should be contacted when the student encounters difficulties in the following areas: employment restrictions, immigration and visa problems, and academic problems.

Handbook on the Placement of Foreign Graduate Students (Graduate Handbook, Part III). Washington, D.C.: National Association for Foreign Student Affairs, 1984.

This third volume of a handbook on the placement of foreign graduate students provides information on schooling in 50 countries and guidelines concerning placement in U. S. graduate programs for each one of them. In addition, country profiles cover: years of study at the primary, secondary, and tertiary levels; diplomas, certificates, and degrees awarded; tertiary institutions, and grading systems. The 50 countries are as follows: Albania, Bahrain, Barbados, Bolivia, Bulgaria, Burundi, Cameroon, Chad, Chile, Cuba, Czechoslovakia, Denmark, Dominican Republic, Ecuador, El Salvador, France, Gabon, Guatemala, Guinea, Jamaica, Kampuchea, Democratic People's Republic of Korea, Lebanon, Malawi, Mali, Mauritania, Mauritius, Niger, Papua/New Guinea, Paraguay, Poland, Romania, Rwanda, Senegal, Sierra Leone, Sri Lanka, Sudan, Surinam, Tanzania, Trinidad/Tobago, Uganda, United Kingdom, Upper Volta, Uruguay, U.S.S.R., Yemen Arab Republic, People's Democratic Republic of Yemen, Yugoslavia, Zaire, and Zimbabwe.

Hjelt, Christine M. and Stewart, Georgia E. *Teaching English As a Second Language: A Guide for the Volunteer Teacher.* Washington, D.C.: National Association for Foreign Student Affairs, 1986. 89 p.

This handbook is designed to provide guidelines for community volunteer teachers of ESL to foreign students' spouses and dependents. It is written in plain English for the volunteer with no prior experience or training in the field. Some information contained is specific and technical -- language training techniques, material selection, and so forth. Other parts are more general or informational -- second language acquisition and the importance of understanding cultural differences when teaching a second language. Materials are based on standard well-established principles of language learning.

How to Live in Britain 1987. The British Council's Guide for Overseas Students and Visitors. London: Macmillan, in association with the British Council, 1987.

Howard, Edrice, ed. *Specialized Study Options U. S. A., 1986-1988. A Guide to Short-Term Educational Programs in the United States for Foreign Nationals. Vol 1: Technical Education,* (2nd edition). New York, NY: Institute of International Education, 1986. 415 p.

Howard, Edrice, ed. *Specialized Study Options U. S. A., 1986-1988. A Guide to Short-Term Educational Programs in the United States for Foreign Nationals. Vol. 2: Professional Development,* (2nd edition). New York, NY: Institute of International Education, 1986. 231 p.

International Students in the United States: A Guide for Secondary School Administrators. Washington, D.C.: National Association for Foreign Student Affairs, 1985.

A secondary school principals' reference guide, this volume provides information on key issues concerning foreign students in the U. S. both in organized exchange programs and under sponsorship of relative and friends. The topics discussed include:

1. elements in promoting successful youth exchange programs
2. admissions and academic placement
3. guidance and counseling
4. profiles of educational systems and cultures of Canada, West Germany, France, Italy, Japan and the United Kingdom.

Appended are United States Information Agency criteria for teenager exchange visitor programs; a list of state consumer protection offices; sample forms to assist in the evaluation of foreign credentials; relevant U. S. immigration regulations, procedures, and forms; and a listing of resource materials and organization.

Jenson, Sharon, et al. *Handbook for Community Organizations Working with Foreign Students: Developing, Maintaining, Revitalizing Programs.* Washington, D.C.: National Association for Foreign Student Affairs, 1986. 30 p.

Focuses on the leadership of volunteers, which remains essential in every type of community organization for foreign student programs. Provides information and suggestions on getting community foreign student programs started, obtaining support and visibility in the community, becoming a functional organization, establishing a hosting program, and developing additional programs. Discusses ways to maintain momentum, publicize, make evaluations and secure help from other sources.

King, Nancy and Huff, Ken. *Host Family Survival Kit: A Guide for American Host Families.* Yarmouth, ME: Intercultural Press, 1985.

Lulat, Y. G. M.; Altbach, Philip G., and Kelly, David H. *Governmental and Institutional Policies on Foreign Students: Analysis, Evaluation and Bibliography.* Buffalo, NY: Comparative Education Center, State University of New York at Buffalo, 1986. 114 p.

A comprehensive bibliography concerning the policy aspects of foreign student affairs is accompanied by a 76-page essay which analyzes the literature on the topic. Both governmental and institutional policy are considered in this publication. Among the topics considered are the policy aspects of the economics of foreign study, the concerns of home (sending) countries, institutional factors relating to foreign students and problems encountered by academic institutions and related issues.

Manek, Suru, et al. *Scholarships for International Students. A Complete Guide to United States Colleges and Universities, 1986-88*, 1st edition. Middleburg Heights, OH: Scholarship Research Group, 1986. 276 p.

National Association for Foreign Student Affairs. *Bibliography on Foreign Student Recruitment*. Washington, D.C.: National Association for Foreign Student Affairs, 1984.

National Association for Foreign Student Affairs. *Foreign Student Admissions -- Bibliography*. Washington D.C.: National Association for Foreign Student Affairs, 1985.

National Association for Foreign Student Affairs. *NAFSA Self-Study Guide*. Washington, D.C.: National Association for Foreign Student Affairs, 1984.

Otto Benecke-Stiftung. *Auslanderstudium in der BRD. Bestandsaufnahme und Bewertung der Literatur (Foreign Study in the FRG: Inventory and Review of the Literature)*. Baden-Baden: NOMOS Verlagsgesellschaft, 1982. 114 p.

This literature review encompasses fifteen commissioned studies, nine dissertations, four other studies, eight conference reports and documentation from the authorities, as well as numerous journal articles. These materials are divided into the following categories: motives, orientation (*Vorinformation*), language proficiency, teaching and learning systems, organization of study, financial situation, adjustment difficulties, academic success, and the implications of foreign study. A summary emphasizes the problems in this area of research, including: a lack of data, unclear goals, limited scope of inquiry and insufficient recognition of the situation in the foreign student's country, all of which make it exceedingly difficult to formulate a comprehensive view of foreign study in the FRG. It also makes it impossible to apply a cost-benefit analysis.

Articles

Baron, Britta and Bachmann, Peter. "Study Abroad in Western Europe: A Bibliography". *European Journal of Education* 22, No. 1 (1987): 101-113.

This bibliography covers study abroad in Western Europe, comprising publications which focus on education, political, psychological aspects of an individual or a group arrangement for a West European student to spend an entire degree course or part of it at a higher education institution in another country. It also includes literature on other topics, such as academic recognition and international higher education cooperation, in cases where such literature is of direct relevance to study abroad. The bibliography is divided into 5 sections: bibliographies; books, studies and monographs; articles; official documents; and dissertations, conference proceedings and other documents.

Lulat, Y. G. M. "International Students and Study Abroad Programs: A Select Bibliography." *Comparative Education Review* 28 (May, 1984): 300-339.

Points out that the literature on international students continues to be dominated by two principal sets of research concerns: those of a sociopsychological character exemplified by studies pertaining to be the cross-cultural consequence of studying abroad and those dealing with how best to help international students to adapt and to succeed in an alien institutional and cultural

environment. Puts forward some questions which merit attention.
Contains a bibliography which is divided into 33 sections.

2. General

Books

Arikpo, Arikpo B. *A Comparison of the Relationship Between
Students' Demographic Characteristics, the Administration of Their
Finances and Their Academic Performance.* Unpublished Ph.D.
Dissertation, University of Nebraska-Lincoln, 1984. 210 p. Order
No. DA8428210

> *Purpose of the Study.* The purpose of the study was to
> investigate the effects that the demographic differences and the
> structural management differences of the quantity and quality of
> financial resources to students from India, Iran, Nigeria, Saudi
> Arabia and Venezuela have on these students' grade point
> averages (GPA) at the University of Nebraska-Lincoln in the
> 1979-83 school years.
>
> *Major Findings.* (1) The most common, yet most unstable forms of
> financial resources to students were employment, family and
> personal funds. (2) University assistantship and home
> government funds were most stable and least available. (3)
> Students with stable funds were Indians and the Saudis, with
> annual expenditures of between $6,001 to $8,000. (4) Students
> with unstable funds were Nigerians and Iranians, with annual
> expenditure of between $8,001 to $10,000. (5) Nationality, level
> of study, marital status, age, family size and categories of
> financial resources each had statistically significant effect upon
> GPA.
>
> *Major Recommendations.* (1) Efforts to sponsor students abroad
> should involve local government districts with a central

coordinating body in each country engaged in international education. (2) The university should base most of its aid to students on need. Other forms of aid should increase over employment. (3) Students should only be allowed to study abroad if sufficiently matured.

Barber, Elinor G., ed. *Foreign Student Flows: Their Significance for American Higher Education.* New York, NY: Institute of International Education, 1985. 129 p.

A report of a conference on foreign student flows to the United States and their implications for American higher education, this volume features two long papers and a summary of the discussion. The papers are Larry Sirowy and Alex Inkeles, "University Level Student Exchanges: The U.S. Role in Global Perspective" and Lewis C. Solmon and Ruth Beddow, "Flows, Costs and Benefits of Foreign Students in the United States: Do We Have a Problem?" Both papers feature statistical information as well as analysis. Among the key findings in the Sirowy-Inkeles paper are:

1. The number of students participating in transnational exchanges has increased eightfold since 1950.
2. Approximately 2/3 of the world's foreign students are sent by the developing countries, while 3/4 of all foreign student enroll in the industrialized nations.
3. In the past decade, Western Europe has restricted the flow of foreign students while the U.S. has maintained an open flow policy. The Soviet Union has tried to attract more foreign students, as has Japan.
4. Fifteen countries account for 60% of the foreign students in the U.S.
5. Thirty percent of the foreign students in the U.S. are enrolled in 1% of the institutions.
6. Undergraduates have come to predominate in the numbers of foreign students in the U.S.

Solmon and Beddow argue that the impact of foreign students on American higher education, in the main, has been small. They make the following additional points:

1. The largest growth of foreign students has been in the fields of business studies and engineering.
2. The proportion of foreign students in the undergraduate population has increased very little and among graduate students from 11 to 16% -- with engineering being an exception to this situation.
3. Foreign undergraduate students tend to cluster at the low selectivity institutions.
4. At all degree levels, the share of foreign degree recipients who pay less than the cost of their education is relatively small, 23% at the bachelor's level, 18% at the master's level and 20.4% at the doctoral level.

Barthel, Sue V. and Early, Julie A., eds. *The International Flow of Scientific and Technical Talent: Data, Policies and Issues.* Washington, D.C.: Scientific Manpower Commission, 1985. 66 p.

Bornsztein, Benjamin. *Why Did They Come? A Study of the Major Factors Which Influence the Foreign Student's Decision to Apply for Admission to Selected Graduate Schools of Education in the United States.* Unpublished Ph.D. Dissertation, University of Minnesota, 1987. 274 p. Order No. DA8710289

This study was guided by the following purposes: (1) to identify the main factors in (a) subjective and objective reasons of foreign students to apply for admission to selected U.S. graduate schools of education, (b) information received and (c) institutional characteristics which influence the decision to apply for admission and to choose one particular institution; (2) to assess the differential influence of those factors in the foreign students' decision; and (3) to analyze the relationships among reasons to apply, usefulness of information received, institutional characteristics in choice of a school, satisfaction with the decision to study in the U.S., and demographic variables such as socioeconomic status, region of origin, and linguistic affiliation.

Data were collected from 393 foreign graduate students of education in 19 campuses of 11 U.S. universities through the use of a 99 items survey questionnaire constructed by the author.

Major findings of the study included most important reasons to apply were "opportunity to increase my professional and academic growth", followed by "availability of advanced educational resources and instructional technology equipment and materials". Informational contacts receiving the highest ratings were "letters, brochures from the university regarding specific programs and "catalogue or university bulletin or publication". Institutional characteristics with the highest ratings as of their degree of description of the chosen institutions were "the curriculum of this school is outstanding in most educational areas" and "... easy availability of educational technology equipment and materials". Significant relationships were found between region of origin and the main scales of the study, socioeconomic status and satisfaction with study in the U.S. Students from "Developing Nations" assigned higher importance to reasons to apply, agreed more in institutional characteristics describing their current institution and found informational contacts more useful than students from the "Developed West".

Briggs, Asa and Burn, Barbara. *Study Abroad: A European and an American Perspective*. Paris: European Institute of Education and Social Policy, 1985. 71 p.

Two overview essays provide a broad perspective on issues relating to study abroad. Asa Briggs, writing from a European perspective, discusses the development of study abroad programs and the current efforts of the European Economic Community to foster student exchanges in Europe. Barbara Burn writes of the issues concerning American student exchanges. She notes that relatively few American students study overseas. Among the problems are:

1. American students do not generally know foreign languages
2. Financial burdens

3. Demographic and enrollment trends in the U.S.
4. Societal and attitudinal deterrents
5. Structural deterrents in American higher education
6. Attitudinal deterrents in American higher education
7. Lack of foreign student services abroad.

Iwao, Sumiko and Shigeru, Hagiwara. *Ryugakusei ga mita Nippon (Japan As Seen by Foreign Students)*. Tokyo: Saimaru Shuppan, 1987. 260 p.

Jones, Philip W. *Australia's International Relations in Education. Australian Education Review* No. 23. Hawthorn: Australian Council for Educational Research, 1986. 122 p.

This special theme issue of the *Australian Education Review* consists of a monograph relating to all aspects of Australia's international education relations by Philip Jones of the University of Sydney. He deals with Australian involvement in regional and international organizations in education, with international educational exchanges including the exchange of materials and personnel and with the bilateral educational assistance programs of the Australian government. The study points out the wide range of Australian involvement in education overseas, particularly in the Southeast Asian and Pacific regions. Of special note to those concerned with foreign students is a chapter on overseas students in Australia. This chapter discusses the historical development of foreign student involvement in Australian universities and colleges and the important policy changes since 1985. Australia is a key host country for foreign students, particularly from Asia, and there have recently been some important debates in Australia concerning this topic. Australia has been particularly concerned about the number of private overseas students.

Kitamura, Kazuyuki. *Daigakukyoiku no Kokusaika -- Sotokara mita Nihon no Daikaku (The Internationalization of Higher Education -- Japan's Universities Seen from Outside)*. Tokyo: Tamagawa University Press, 1984. 254 p.

Lampton, David M. *A Relationship Restored: Trends in U.S.-China Educational Exchanges, 1978-1984.* Washington, D.C.: National Academy Press, 1986.

A full-scale study of the various ramifications of U.S.-China academic exchange. This volume deals with the history of academic relationships between the two countries, the characteristics of exchange participants, the nature and scope of exchange programs, language training in both Chinese and English, campus issues related to China-U.S. exchanges and the consequences of exchanges for selected academic disciplines. This data-based study provides key information and perspectives.

Report of the Australian Government Education Mission to South-East Asia and Hong Kong. Canberra: Australian Government Publishing Service, 1985.

Research Institute for Higher Education, Hiroshima University. *Higher Education Expansion in Asia.* Hiroshima: 1985. 180 p.

Expansion of the past 10 years in Asian higher education and associated problems, as well as the role of colleges and universities in national development, are discussed in 11 papers from a 1985 international seminar. In particular, the papers address respectively the prospects and problems in higher education in China, Indonesia, Japan, Korea, Malaysia, the Philippines, and Thailand. The volume ends with papers by W. K. Cummings and J. Hicks, dealing respectively with Asian overseas students' preference for the U.S. and the situation of Asian students in Japan.

Sirowy, Larry and Inkeles, Alex. *University-Level Student Exchanges: The U.S. Role in Global Perspective.* New York, NY: Institute of International Education, 1985.

One of the best overviews of all aspects of foreign student trends, policies and developments, this 85-page essay presents useful statistical information as well as careful analysis of trends. Most of the statistics are valid for 1981 or earlier, so very current information is not available. Among the generalizations presented are:

•The proportion of foreign students in the U.S. student population (2.6%) is significantly lower than for France (12%), Britain (11%) or West Germany (5.6%).
•Foreign students are more likely than domestic students to study in engineering or medical sciences rather than in the humanities or social sciences.
•For a few Third World nations, a very large percentage of their total student populations are studying outside the nation.
•There are considerable regional variations in foreign student flows. For example, the majority of foreign students in the U.S. are from Asia, but in France most foreign students are from Africa.
•There are significant changes in the countries of origin for foreign students over time. Canada for many years was the largest sending country to the U.S. It was replaced by Iran, and now Taiwan, Malaysia and China are among the most important sending nations.
•After having increased dramatically for a number of years in the U.S., the numbers of foreign students have remained relatively steady for several years, with only modest growth.
•Women tend to be underrepresented in foreign student populations.
•The majority of foreign students studying in the U.S. are undergraduates, but it is felt that this might be a temporary phenomenon and a balance of half graduate students and half undergraduates may soon be reestablished.

Solmon, Lewis C. and Young, Betty J. *The Foreign Student Factor: Impact on American Higher Education*. New York, NY: Institute of International Education, 1987. 95 p.

This unique report focuses on the attitudes of foreign students in the United States and on detailed statistical information concerning foreign students in American colleges and universities. The data bases are the annual freshmen attitude surveys collected by the Cooperative Institutional Research Program

(CIRP) and the Higher Education General Information Survey (HEGIS), the national statistical data base on higher education. While the attitude material relates only to foreign undergraduate students, it is nonetheless a unique source of information. Indeed, this volume is a key resource, since it uses the most comprehensive sources of data in the areas of its concern and it provides a detailed analysis of these two data bases. The information and analysis provided will be of considerable relevance to anyone concerned with foreign student policy or administration.

Among the findings are the following:

•Foreign students tend to be older than U.S. students.
•Foreign students tend to have more left wing or liberal attitudes than their U.S. counterparts, but the attitude configuration has become more conservative during the 1980s.
•An often neglected group in the student population are resident aliens, who are not "officially" foreign students but who fit many of the characteristics of foreign students.
•Foreign students tend to come from affluent families.
•Foreign students, in their choice of places to study, place greater stress on academic quality than do American students and are less concerned with the cost of education. They are, however, more concerned with the availability of scholarship aid.
•The West and Southwest have attracted the largest number of foreign students and the Southeast has shown the largest increases in recent years.
•Foreign students aspire to go beyond the bachelor's degree in their studies.

Wobbekind, Richard L. *A Reconsideration of Foreign Student Demand for U.S. Higher Education.* Unpublished Ph.D. Dissertation, University of Colorado at Boulder, 1984. 152 p. Order No. DA8428693

Foreign students have been attending colleges and universities in the United States at rapidly increasing rates since the late 1960s. Due to a variety of factors including demographic changes and cost considerations, U.S. universities have been more than willing to accept this increasing group of foreign students. Many U.S. universities have grown dependent on a large foreign student population, particularly in graduate programs. With no change in the current trends projected, both university and government officials are interested in the causal links behind increasing foreign student enrollments.

Although the non-return of U.S. educated foreign nationals is an equally important issue, this study makes no attempt to address that issue. Rather, the attempt here is to: (1) identify key variables in foreign student demand for higher education, and (2) test the predictive power of a theoretical model of educational demand.

Articles

Agarwal, Vinod B. and Winkler, Donald R. "Foreign Demand for United States Higher Education: A Study of Developing Countries in the Eastern Hemisphere". *Economic Development and Cultural Change* 33, No. 3 (April, 1985): 623-644.

This article sets forth a model of foreign demand for U.S. higher education and estimates that model for several countries using time-series data for 1954-73. Countries selected are low- or middle-income nations in the Eastern Hemisphere. The paper first presents the theory of student demand for U.S. higher education. Next it specifies the model and explains the estimation procedure, followed by a detailed discussion of the data and some of its problems. Lastly, the estimated demand equations are presented, the results discussed, and the policy implications evaluated.

Agarwal, V. B. and Winkler, D. R. "Migration of Foreign Students to the United States". *Journal of Higher Education* 56 (September/October, 1985): 509-522.

During the past 25 years, foreign students have increasingly chosen to come to the U.S.A. for higher education. Although the reliability of available data is open for debate, documentation provides a reasonably accurate composite view of the migration process, including determinants of student flow and changes in the countries of origin. Whether or not the foreign student enrollment trend will continue depends in part on how American colleges relate to declines in domestic enrollments and on how much appeal American higher education continues to hold for foreign students.

Altbach, Philip G. "The Foreign Student Dilemma". *Teachers College Record* 87 (Summer, 1986): 590-610.

This article discusses foreign students in a comparative framework. It examines the role of the sending countries and their policies, the receiving nations, broader patterns and flows of foreign students and the policy implications related to foreign study. A section considers the role of dependency when related to foreign study. The author relates the phenomenon of foreign study to broader developments in international policies and considers the topic from the perspective of international knowledge flows. The author believes that there are both costs and benefits to foreign study and that those involved should be aware of both.

Altbach, P. G. and Lulat, Y. G. M. "International Students in Comparative Perspective: Toward a Political Economy of International Study". In *Research on Foreign Students and International Study*, eds. P. Altbach, D. Kelly, and Y. Lulat (New York: Praeger, 1985): 1-65.

A detailed essay discussing the literature on foreign students and international study from a range of disciplinary and other perspectives. Among the topics considered are economic cost-benefit analysis of foreign study, issues of advising and counseling foreign students, language proficiency, curriculum and foreign students, the relevance of international study, student flow issues and others. The authors argue that a multi-disciplinary approach is necessary for a thorough understanding of the complex issues relating to foreign study.

Bergen, Timothy J., Jr. and Kelley, Loretta M. "International Education: Toward the Future". *International Education* 15, No. 1 (1985): 5-8.

Boaz, Martha. "International Education: An Imperative Need". *Journal of Education for Library and Information Science* 26, No. 3 (Winter, 1986): 165-173.

Coombs, Philip H. "Changes in Foreign Student Flows and Policies". In *The World Crisis in Education: The View from the Eighties*, ed. P. Coombs (New York: Oxford University Press, 1985): 314-328.

This chapter examines changes in the pattern of foreign student flow during 1970-80 and in the policies of several major host countries. Questions addressed include: Where did all foreign students come from? Where did they go to study? How were they financed? What did they study and at what levels? How did the receiving countries react? What new factors enter the picture that are likely to influence the size and pattern of foreign student flows in the future? What policy issues and options face sending countries and host countries?

Cummings, William K. "Going Overseas for Higher Education: The Asian Experience". *Comparative Education Review* 28 (May, 1984): 241-257.

Analyzes the national differences in the numbers of students the selected Asian countries send abroad for higher education. Points out that the increasing interdependence of national economies resulting in the weakening of national boundaries on labor markets may play an important role in motivating people to seek overseas study, but indigenous forces have the predominant influence on the demand for overseas study. Finds that essentially unpredictable economic and political developments have considerable impact on the flow of students overseas and these exceptional developments in some instances stimulate and in others brake the volume and direction.

Ebuchi, Kazukimi. "Recent Trends in Foreign Student Research in the United States: With Special Reference to the Impact of International Student Flow". *Research in Higher Education (Daigaku Ronshu)* No. 17 (1987): 25-45.

Exodus West. *Asiaweek* 11 (March 1, 1985): 21-30.

> A detailed discussion of the nature and problems of students from Asia studying in the West. Statistics concerning the flow of students, the amounts of money spent by Asian nations and related items are provided. There is, in addition, a discussion of the adaptation problems of Asian students in the West, pointing to difficulties in social interaction patterns. Most Asian students are interested in engineering or management study, and they seem to work hard and generally do well in their studies. Countries like Malaysia, Singapore, Hong Kong, South Korea and Taiwan, which send large numbers of students overseas to the industrialized nations, have been particularly concerned about the cost of overseas study and issues such as return rates.

Fasheh, Munir. "Foreign Students in the United States: An Enriching Experience or a Wasteful One?" *Contemporary Educational Psychology* 9, No. 3 (July, 1984): 313-320.

> Problems that international students deal with as they adjust to living in the U.S. are presented, and their implications for mutual cooperation once students return to their homelands are discussed. Some practical steps that might be taken to relieve many of the problems described are suggested.

"Foreign Students: A Valuable Link". *Change* 19 (July-August, 1987): 39-43.

Goodman, N. G. "The International Institutionalization of Education". In *Bridges to Knowledge: Foreign Students in Comparative Education*, eds. E. Barber, P. Altbach, and R. Myers (Chicago: University of Chicago Press, 1984): 7-18.

Goodman places international students and educational exchange in the context of world systems analysis and argues that such exchanges must be understood in the context of international inequalities in education. This is particularly important because about 80% of the world's foreign students come from the Third World and study in the industrialized nations. Data from Malaysia are used to illustrate the main points.

Güclüol, K. "Third World Students in Advanced Countries". *Higher Education in Europe* 11, No. 3 (1986): 31-35.

This article focuses on the problems faced by Third World students in developed countries. The article emphasizes the fact that higher education institutions in developed countries should become more sensitive to such problems as screening and selection, language difficulties, lack of orientation, selection of school, adjustment to a new culture, and readjustment to the home country, financing, and, finally, brain drain.

Hayhoe, Ruth. "Sino-Western Educational Cooperation: History and Perspectives". *Prospects* 15, No. 2 (1985): 251-261.

The article focuses on educational values and their transformation in the modernization process, especially values relating to the structure and distribution of knowledge in the higher curricular system. First, the Chinese tradition in higher education is considered, including the challenge it presents to its modernizers. German, American, and French intergovernmental projects of the early decades are analyzed comparatively to see how they contributed to Chinese educational modernization. The second part deals with contemporary projects of cooperation with each of these countries on Chinese soil. To illustrate Sino-Western cooperation in education, five universities -- Qinghua University, Tongji University and Wuhan University, Dalian Institute of Technology, and Nanjing University -- are discussed as examples of bilateral collaboration.

He, Dongchang. "China's Educational Interaction with Foreign Countries -- Review and Prospects". *Chinese Education* 21 (Spring, 1988): 20-24.

Johnson, Duska. "Home Students of Foreign Origin". *New Community* 12 (Summer, 1985): 266-272.

Kitamura, Kazuyuki. "The Internationalization of the University". *Research in Higher Education (Daigaku Ronshu)* No. 15 (1986): 9-14.

Talks about the need and the problems of internationalizing the universities of Japan. The article was prepared as an introductory report for the International Symposium on University Internationalization and Foreign Students held in Hiroshima, Japan, in 1986. Japan's educational system has developed first by Westernizing the system, and by "Japanizing" it later. As Japan's economy developed and began to play a major role in the world market, the closed nature of its educational system has been criticized both from within and outside the country. Argues about the internationalization of Japanese universities in terms of their academic standard, institutional condition to promote scholarly exchange, and the attitude of the people towards foreign students and faculties. Points out that it is important for the country to learn from neighboring countries to promote the internationalization of universities.

Marion, Paul B. "Research on Foreign Students at Colleges and Universities in the United States". In *Guiding the Development of Foreign Students*, ed. K. Pyle (San Francisco, London: Jossey-Bass, 1986): 65-82.

Reviews research on foreign students. The summary points include: (a) foreign students' academic achievement is similar to that of American students, and there is a positive correlation between English language ability and academic success; (b) the adjustment of foreign students to the U.S. is affected by a variety of factors, and differs from student to student; (c) academic achievement of foreign students affects and is affected by their attitudes and adjustment; and (d) academic training received in the U.S. is generally perceived to be useful to students upon returning home, and returned students undergo a readjustment process in the home country similar to that experienced during their stay in the host country.

Marris, R. "The Paradox of Services". *Political Quarterly* 56 (July/September, 1985): 242-252.

Okihara, Yutaka. "Issues and Problems Concerning the Foreign Student Increase". *Research in Higher Education (Daigaku Ronshu)* (In Japanese) No. 15 (1986): 155-157.

Opper, Susan. "Students: Nailed to the Bench or Studying Abroad?" *European Journal of Education* 22, No. 1 (1987): 27-38.

Who takes the initiative in an institution of higher education to get a foreign study program off the ground? What motivates them to do so? Do national and supra-national policies which promote study abroad have any effect at the practical level of academic program development? These are the questions this article pursues, and it does it from primarily a European perspective. The article is in the form of a preliminary highlight on these issues based on findings from an ongoing Study Abroad Evaluation Project. Detailed analyses are presented elsewhere in the reports issued by the evaluation project.

Selvaratnam, V. "The International Flow of Scholars and Students: A Vehicle for Cross-Cultural Understanding, International Co-operation and Global Development?" *International Journal of Educational Development* 5, No. 4 (1985): 307-323.

Outlines the impetus for the origin and development of the international flow of scholars and students in a global context. Examines the implications and contributions this movement makes towards cross-cultural understanding, international co-operation in higher education and a global development in knowledge. Analyses the educational, cultural and economic advantages and disadvantages that sending and host countries have derived and continue to derive from these flows. Points out that the benefits outweigh the disadvantages, particularly in the light of the growing new international economic order accompanied by an interdependent world economic system and that the fact that a number of developed host countries have introduced a series of protectionist measures to curtail the number of overseas students coming into their institutions of higher education has adversely affected the poorer developing countries and their students.

Shorrock, H. C. "Policies and Issues Concerning the Receiving and Sending of Foreign Students: The Current American Situation". *Research in Higher Education (Daigaku Ronshu)* No. 15 (1986): 111-141.

The article gives some useful statistics about America's receiving and sending of foreign students. It then analyzes the trends in U.S. foreign student enrollment by major fields of study, academic level, gender, and costs and sources of funding. It also discusses the United States' policy toward foreign students at federal, state, as well as institutional levels. In the discussion on U.S.-Japan students exchanges, the article focuses on the key issues of qualifications and selection of students and the aftercare of these students. The concluding section analyzes the factors that have caused the asymmetrical patterns in the American foreign student exchange situation and offers some thought on the internationalization of Japan's higher education.

Uzzell, David. "A Co-orientation Analysis of the Professional Placement in Europe". *European Journal of Education* 22, No. 1 (1987): 85-100.

This study uses a co-orientation model to explore the simultaneous perceptions of the professional placement abroad by language students and staff. The results demonstrate conclusively that there is not one consensual view concerning placement abroad -- not only do students assess the objectives and the achievement of objectives differently from the staff, but also differently among themselves, depending upon the stage they are at in their university career. The study also finds the general level of dissatisfaction among the third-year students. Although the research focuses on language undergraduates working in France as part of their degree course, it is suggested that the theoretical position, the methodology and the conclusion here have relevance for both the assessment of professional placement in other curriculum areas and student exchange programs.

Weiler, Hans N. "The Political Dilemmas of Foreign Study". *Comparative Education Review* 28 (May, 1984): 168-179.

Analyzes the fundamental ambivalence in the relationship between the universities of North America and the countries of the Third World which is reflected in serious dilemmas for both the institutions of higher education in the U.S. and the political and professional leadership in the countries of the Third World. Argues that these dilemmas will tend to become more acute as the enrollment of foreign students in U.S. institutions grows. Stresses that as long as North American universities continue to train academics and professionals from the countries of the world's periphery, they will continue to confer on them statuses which make those students part of a very distinct and remarkably persistent upper class in their own societies and will help exacerbate the already intractable problem of social equality in those countries. Some propositions on what those elements might be which would moderate the role played by the American universities in sustaining the relationship of cultural dependence between center and periphery are offered.

Williams, Gareth. "The International Market for Overseas Students in the English-Speaking World". *Journal of Education* 22, No. 1 (1987): 15-25.

The educational, social and economic implications of Britain's recently adopted policy of charging foreign students for the full cost of their education are examined, especially in the context of the worldwide demand for higher education in English-language institutions.

Williams, P. "Making Tomorrow Happen Sooner: Towards a More Equal International Exchange of Students, Teachers, and Research". In *Education and Development*, ed. R. Garrett (London: Croom Helm, 1984): 321-343.

> A discussion of the pros and cons of international study, with a stress on providing an appropriate balance of relevance and interest for Third World students. Williams points out the negative aspects of international study and discusses the need for better international student programs. He argues, for example, for joint North-South planning of international study courses, more in-country courses taught by Northern scholars in Third World nations, joint cooperation among institutions in North and South for research and collaboration and other improvements in the status quo. The chapter concludes with a number of recommendations for the British government regarding overseas students.

Yamashiro, M. "The Big Welcome for Foreign College Students". *Japan Quarterly* 34 (January/March, 1987): 39-45.

3. Statistical Materials

Books

Closing the Doors?: A Statistical Report on International Students in Canada 1983-85. Ottawa: Canadian Bureau of International Education, 1986.

> A comprehensive report on trends on foreign study in Canada between 1983 and 1985. The report argues that Canada, through its policies relating to foreign study, is closing off opportunities and that this is in the long run detrimental to Canadian policy and Canadian higher education. Among the findings are:

•Foreign student number declined by 17% during the period.
•54% of the students were at the university level.
•Foreign students decline as a proportion of the total Canadian university population from 5.3% in 1982 to 4.9% in 1985.
•Foreign student numbers increased in the two provinces that did not impose differential fees (Manitoba and Saskatchewan).
•Foreign students came predominantly from the "Group of Ten" Asian countries and mostly from countries with high GNPs.
•At the university level, students tended to concentrate in such fields as mathematics, physical sciences and engineering.

The report makes a number of recommendations aimed at reversing Canada's decline as a focus for international study.

Koester, Jolene. *A Profile of the U.S. Student Abroad*, New York: Council on International Educational Exchange, 1985.

The first in a projected series which documents the results of a nationwide surveys of U.S. students who study, travel and work abroad. The results of this survey provides a statistical information base of the U.S. students who cross international boundaries. Demographic characteristics of these students, and a description of their intended international experience, attitude, and behavioral characteristics are also included. In addition, students having a prior international experience provide a self-assessment of the impact of that experience. Presents findings related to recurring patterns in (1) relationship between language study and the international student, (2) parental language and international residence, (3) career goals and international experience, (4) the length of time of the student's international trips, (5) notable number of high school students travelling, (6) increasing number of students from business, sciences, engineering and the professions interested in international travel, and (7) significant number of students receiving scholarship/grant support.

Von Zur-Muehlen, Max. *International Students in Canada: A Statistical Portrait of the Mid-1980's.* Ottawa, Ontario: Canadian Higher Education Research Network, 1987. (Working Paper 87-2.) 88 p.

Williams, Gareth; Woodhall, Maureen, and O'Brien, Una. *Overseas Students and their Place of Study: Report of a Survey.* London: Overseas Students Trust, 1986. 100 p.

The result of a large scale survey of foreign students in British universities and polytechnics and interviews with officials of postsecondary institutions, the following findings are among those included in this report:

1. There has been a drop in the numbers of overseas students from several countries, notably Malaysia, and an increase from the countries of the European Economic Community.
2. There has been an increase in the proportion of students receiving support from British sources to about 25% from 14% in 1980. However, about 3/4 of the students felt that they did not have adequate support for their studies.
3. About 90% of the students felt satisfied with their courses and about 30% were very satisfied. About 3/4 felt that they were getting good educational value for the money spent.
4. Loneliness and home-sickness are widespread, as is a felling of isolation from the British people. These feelings were particularly strong from students from Africa and the Middle East.
5. British academic institutions have increased their entrepreneurial activity since 1980, and many universities now rely on foreign students for 5 to 10 % of their income.
6. There has been an increase in the courses offered which are designed to attract foreign students.
7. The majority of higher education institutions offer some English language and study skills training to foreign students.

Williams, Gareth; Woodhall, M., and O'Brien, U. *The Overseas Students (Appendix A to "Overseas Students and Their Place of Study"*. London: Overseas Students Trust, 1986. 200 p.

This study describes a survey of overseas students in British higher and further education and the institutions where they study. The appendix describes the characteristics of foreign students studying in Britain. It deals with such topics as the main demographic characteristics of overseas students, reasons for studying in Britain, levels of financial support, financial problems of students, views of overseas students concerning their study and other aspects of life in Britain, special issues of women students and related matters. The report provides detailed statistical information and is one of the most complete sources of information concerning finances, student numbers, and attitudes available for any country.

Williams, Gareth; Woodhall, M., and O'Brien, U. *The Institutions (Appendix B to "Overseas Students and their Place of Study"*. London: Overseas Students Trust, 1986. 198 p.

This appendix volume of a large scale study of "Overseas Students and Their Place of Study" deals with the institutions at which foreign students in Britain study. It deals with publicly funded institutions (including all of the universities and the polytechnics) and also with privately funded institutions (such as English language institutions, vocational institutions and the like). This is the first study which has collected a significant amount of information on privately funded educational institutions, which have been the cause of considerable controversy in Britain because of recruiting policies and other issues. Among the topics considered in the survey are recruitment policy of both public and private institutions, admissions procedures, English language requirements, credit transfer and related topics. This is one of the largest surveys of the relationship between institutions and foreign students done in Britain.

Wilson, Kenneth M. *The TOEFL Native Country File: Detailed Data on Candidate Populations, 1977-79.* Princeton, NJ: Educational Testing Service, 1981.

Zikopoulos, Marianthi, ed. *Open Doors 1985-1986: Report on International Education Exchange.* New York, NY: Institute of International Education, 1986.

Zikopoulos, Marianthi and Barber, Elinor G., eds. *Profiles: Detailed Analyses of the Foreign Student Population, 1983-1984.* New York, NY: Institute of International Education, 1985.

> This volume is a report of a survey done every two years by the Institute of International Education of American academic institutions concerning foreign students. It provides overall information on numbers of foreign students at each institution, specialities being studied by foreign students on a national basis, differentiation between graduate and undergraduate students, and similar data. Regional information is also provided, as well as a national breakdown of foreign students studying in the United States.

Articles

Department of Education and Science. "Students from Abroad in Great Britain in 1982-83 and Provisional Information for 1983-84". *Department of Education and Science: Statistical Bulletin* No. 7 (June, 1984): 1-12.

"Foreign Students in the Countries of the Europe Region: Basic Statistical Data". *Higher Education in Europe* 11, No. 1 (1986): 68-79.

> This article provides basic statistical data relative to the flow of foreign students in Europe, based on data drawn from the UNESCO statistical yearbooks for 1983 and 1984. The data are grouped in three main tables. Table 1 follows the evolution of the total student enrollment in Europe over 1980-83. Table 2 breaks down the total number of foreign students by their region

of origin, while Table 3 indicates the number of foreign students received in each European country, and the number of European scholars sent abroad to pursue higher education during the same period.

Goosens, Gérard. "Statistiques Relatives aux élèves étrangers en Belgique Francophone (Statistics Relative to Foreign Students in French Speaking Belgium)". *Revue Belge de Psychologie et de Pédogogie* 45 (March-June, 1983): 15-18.

"Two Trends of Change Among Shanghai's Returned Scholars". *Chinese Education* 21 (Spring, 1988): 97-103.

4. Historical Studies

Books

Abe, Hiroshi, ed. *Beityukyoiku Koryu no Kiseki -- Kokusai Bunkakyoryoku no Rekisitekikyokun_ (A Historical Pattern of U.S. - China International Exchange -- Historical Lessons of an International Cultural Exchange)*. Tokyo: Kazankai, 1985. 471 p.

Breitenbach, Dieter. *Auslandsausbildung als Gegenstand sozial- wissenschaftlicher Forschung (Study Abroad As an Object of Social Science Research)*. Saarbrucken: Verlag der SSIP-Schriften, 1973. 465 p.

This dissertation is the first comprehensive representation and analysis of previous research on study abroad written in German since 1945. The study traces the development of the field, methodological aspects of the research, cultural comparisons, etc. The concepts of adjustment and cultural transfer are also dealt with. In the appendix are five case studies of cultural adjustment of practitioners from developing countries similar to those which involve students.

Burke, Ardath W., ed. *The Modernizers: Overseas Students, Foreign Employees and Meiji Japan.* Boulder, CO: Westview, 1985. p. 431.

This volume of essays by Japanese and Western scholars sheds light on the process of modernization in 19th century Japan, focusing on two significant aspects of Japan's transition to a modern society: the decision to live for a time with the necessary evil of relying on the skill and advice of foreign employees and the decision to dispatch Japanese students overseas. The essays make clear that the success of both these programs went beyond aiding Japan's modernization goals; their indirect effects often extended much further than planned, influencing even today the fields of education, science and history, and affecting other countries' knowledge of Japan.

Dudden, Arthur P. and Dynes, Russell R., eds. *The Fulbright Experience, 1946-1986.* New Brunswick, NJ: Transaction Books, 1986.

Idris, Safwan. *Tokoh - Tokoh National: Overseas Education and the Evolution of the Indonesian Educated Elite.* Ph.D. Dissertation, The University of Wisconsin - Madison, 1982. 454 p. Order No. DA8301867

This study seeks to understand the development of the modern Indonesian educated elite. The study is based on the analysis and comparison of about seventy prominent Indonesian leaders from five sub-generations. Born between 1890 and 1940, each sub-generation represents a ten-year birth cohort, based on generations at twenty-year intervals. The three generations are identified as the '1928', '1945', and '1966' generations.

To summarize, the development of the elite since the turn of the century is characterized by the growing nationalist consciousness among the 1908 generation, the rising revolution orientation among the 1928 and the first phase of the 1945 generations and the rising conservatism among the last phase of the 1945 and the early phase of the 1966 generations. The conservatism of the two groups seems to have contributed to the regeneration problem faced by the current generation.

Several tendencies can be identified in the elite ideological development. The mediation of overseas experiences by ethnic factors is reflected in the syncretic orientation among the Javanese and liberal orientation among the non-Javanese. Among the new ideologies, Islamic reformism, being mediated by the early establishment of Islam in Indonesia, has developed on a sustained basis. The ability of a new ideology to endure an assimilation process is important for the continuity or decline of the elite group associated with the ideology. Conflicts such as between the Muslims and the secular nationalists is reflective of the imperialist objective associated with the education of the elite.

Articles

Burks, A. "Japan's Outreach: The Ryugakusei". In *The Modernizers: Overseas Students, Foreign Employees and Meiji Japan*, ed. A. Burks (Boulder, CO: Westview Press, 1985): 145-169.

Ishizuki, M. "Overseas Study by Japanese in the Early Meiji Period". In *The Modernizers: Overseas Students, Foreign Employees and Meiji Japan*, ed. A. Burks (Boulder, CO: Westview Press, 1985): 161-186.

A consideration of the impact and destinations of Japanese students who went abroad for study after the Meiji restoration in 1868. The chapter discusses the policy of the government, motivations for overseas study, numbers and destinations of students (the total up to 1874 was 575 students, with slightly under half going to the United States and other large groups studying in Britain and Germany). The chapter concludes with several case studies of students and a discussion of the influence of these students on Japanese academic development.

Pennacchio, Luigi G. "Toronto's Public Schools and the Assimilation of Foreign Students, 1900-1920". *Journal of Educational Thought* 20, No. 1 (April, 1986): 37-48.

The article describes the policy of Toronto's public schools toward foreign students during the pre-World War I era as promoting their assimilation into the city's Protestant, British-Canadian cultural milieu. It also considers the roles played by educators, Protestant missionaries, and society in general in the assimilative efforts, and the attempts of foreigners to preserve their cultures.

Wu, Genliang. "The Historical Role of Returned Students in Modern China". *Chinese Education* 21 (Spring, 1988): 16-19.

5. Policy of "Sending" Countries

Articles

Hayhoe, Ruth. "A Comparative Analysis of Chinese-Western Academic Exchange". *Comparative Education* 20, No. 1 (1984): 39-56.

The article sets forth China's policies concerning Chinese-Western academic exchange. It examines the Sino-European scholarly exchange situation by noting the different approaches toward scholarly exchanges in Britain, France, and West Germany. American, Canadian, and Japanese exchange policies and programs are also reviewed in contrast to the Sino-European scene. Stress is put on identifying policies that are likely to contribute to cultural and educational autonomy and those that might increase hazards of dependency.

Khasawnik, Sami A. "Science Policy in the Arab World". *International Review of Education* 32, No. 1 (1986): 55-70.

Kim, Ran Soo. "Korean Policy for Sending Students Abroad". *Research in Higher Education (Daigaku Ronshu)* No. 15 (1986): 95-101.

Liu, Sheng-Chi. "Communist China's Overseas Study Policy Since 1978". *Issues and Studies* 21 (August, 1985): 73-103.

China has sent a large number of scholars and students to study in foreign countries, in particular to the U.S., Japan, and Western Europe. The emphasis is on learning advanced science and technology. This indicates that China's policy of sending students abroad is ancillary to the state objective of promoting the four modernizations. Because of the poor national economy and the shortage of foreign exchange reserves, the budget for sending government-sponsored students abroad has been limited.

McBeth, J. "The Student Riddle: Thais Tighten Control Over Who Studies in the Soviet Union". *Far Eastern Economic Review* 130 (November 21, 1985): 38.

Rajendran, M. "Malaysia's Policy of Foreign Students". *Research in Higher Education (Daigaku Ronshu)* No. 15 (1986): 103-110.

Having introduced the policy of the Malaysian government towards students studying abroad, the author discusses at length the major problems encountered by the government and some of the deficiencies in the administration of student affairs abroad by government officials. The problems discussed include the imposition of higher fees by some developed countries, the emergence of Islamic extremism and radical chauvinism among many Malaysian students abroad, and the problem of chauvinism among some Malaysian students of Malay, Chinese, and Indian origin who study abroad. A brief discussion on the status of foreign students in Malaysia is also included. To conclude, the author gives some pointers as to the measures that could be taken by the government on the issue of Malaysian students abroad.

"What Are the New Government Regulations with Regard to Sending People to Study Abroad". *Chinese Education* 21 (Spring, 1988): 29-34.

6. Policy of "Host" Countries

Books

Chandler, Alice. *Foreign Students and Government Policy: Britain, France and Germany.* Washington, D.C.: American Council on Education, 1985.

> Dr. Chandler, a senior administrator at the State University of New York, provides an overview of foreign student policy in three key Western European nations. She discusses the broader configurations of policy development relating to foreign students. She points out that current British policy, which emphasizes full-fees for foreign students, has meant problems for higher education institutions. French policy has been more receptive to foreign students, but current discussions may mean closer controls and governmental policies aimed at regulating the numbers of students. The Federal Republic of Germany has remained the most international in its policies concerning foreign students.

Commonwealth Secretariat. *Britain's Policy on Overseas Students.* London: Commonwealth Standing Committee on Student Mobility, Commonwealth Secretariat, 1985.

Commonwealth Secretariat. *Canada's Policy on Overseas Students.* London: Commonwealth Standing Committee on Student Mobility, Commonwealth Secretariat, 1985.

Commonwealth Secretariat. *Commonwealth Student Mobility: A Way Forward* (4th Report). London: Commonwealth Standing Committee on Student Mobility, Commonwealth Secretariat, 1985. 58 p.

> For several years, the Commonwealth has had as one of its major education concerns the issue of student mobility among the Commonwealth nations. At its 1985 meeting, the following recommendations were made to encourage such mobility:

•The Commonwealth should formulate specific policies relating to students mobility;
•There should be a non-discrimination policy with regard to student fees;
•Fees should be at less than "full cost";
•Intra-Commonwealth student exchanges should be given more emphasis.

Commonwealth Secretariat. *New Zealand's Policy on Overseas Students*. London: Commonwealth Standing Committee on Student Mobility, Commonwealth Secretariat, 1985.

Hambly, F. S. *Australian Overseas Student Policy*. London: Commonwealth Standing Committee on Student Mobility, Commonwealth Secretariat, 1985.

McCann, William J., Jr. *A Survey of Policy Changes: Foreign Students in Public Institutions of Higher Education from 1983 to 1985*. IEE Research Report No. 8. New York, NY: Institute of International Education, 1986. 14 p.

The author reports the following results based on a survey of 681 public colleges and universities:

1. With annual percentage increases below 1%, most colleges had stable (42%) or declining (30%) foreign enrollment since 1983.
2. A third of the schools did not maintain foreign student services at fully adequate levels because of financial constraints, lack of interest in foreign students, and personnel and office space shortages.
3. Many schools were revising English test score requirements, and 43% of the schools indicated that admission standards for foreign student have become stiffer than those for domestic students.
4. About half of the schools required foreign students to demonstrate their ability to cover their educational expenses before admission.

Mutual Advantage: Report of the Committee of Review of Private Overseas Student Policy. Canberra: Australian Government Publishing Service, 1984. 406 p.

The growth in the numbers of privately funded foreign students in Australia has been an issue of concern to Australian policymakers and educators. The report finds that the distinction between officially sponsored students and private students is often artificial and recommends that the Australian government recognize its role as a major host for overseas students and plan more adequately for students from the Third World, both funded and unfunded. Recommendations deal with a variety of specific policies for both government agencies and academic institutions.

The Next Steps. London: Overseas Students Trust, 1986. 92 p.

This comprehensive volume reports the results of a major British inquiry into foreign student policy. It describes the various British programs to assist foreign students in the U.K. in the aftermath of the "full fee" policy that was implemented in 1979, which the report feels was a disaster for British interests as well as for foreign students in Britain. The report argues that there must be an increase in public funds devoted to foreign students and argues that this is important for broader foreign policy and economic reasons. It discusses the post-1983 selective assistance schemes and feels that these were a step in the right direction. The report argues that it will be possible to build on recent improvements and to enhance help for foreign students without major additional funding. The document ends with a very useful set of appendices that provide statistics relating to foreign students and foreign student policies in a number of countries.

North-South Institute. *Foreign Students in Canada: A Neglected Foreign Policy Issue.* Ottawa: North-South Institute, 1985. 12 p.

Ontario Government. *Ontario Universities: Options and Futures (Report of the Commission on the Future Development of*

Universities in Ontario). Toronto, Ontario: Government of Ontario, 1985.

Shotnes, Stephen, ed. *International Comparisons in Overseas Student Affairs: Papers Arising from the 1985 UKCOSA Annual Conference.* London: United Kingdom Council on Overseas Student Affairs, 1986.

> A series of eight country-based papers focusing on foreign student policies and the situation of foreign students in that country. The countries considered are Australia, Belgium, Canada, West Germany, India, Ireland, the Netherlands, and the United States. A final chapter explores the implications of these papers for Britain. While the focus is on foreign student policy, each paper provides useful statistical information concerning foreign student numbers and trends. Financial information, for example, relating to fees for study by foreign students is also provided.

Towards a Policy on International Education. London: United Kingdom Council on Overseas Students Affairs, 1986.

> This forty-page volume is a collection of position papers sponsored by the United Kingdom Council on Overseas Student Affairs that argue for the importance of international education and particularly for the positive role of overseas students in British education and society. The papers were prepared in response to the British government's imposition of the "full fee" policy for overseas students in 1980. The topics dealt within these papers are: The Importance of the International Perspective in a Strategy for Higher Education, The Need for a Responsible Recruitment Policy, International Relations and Overseas Students, Targeted Schemes of Support for Overseas Students, and Britain and Commonwealth Student Mobility. All of the papers argue that a commitment to international education will benefit British foreign policy, higher education, and the students themselves.

Working Group on Educational Assistance to Refugees. *The Forgotten Overseas Students: Towards a Policy for Refugees*. London: World University Service, 1986.

The plight of the growing numbers of foreign students in Britain who are refugees is examined in this report from the World University Service. The report identifies students from such countries as Namibia, South Africa, Ethiopia. Among the recommendations made are:

•Institutions should set up mechanisms for dealing with financial and other problems of refugee students, for advising such students, and for permitting them to pursue part-time study;
•Various social service agencies that deal with refugees should work with academic institutions on problems concerning refugee students;
•Special scholarships should be set up to help bring refugee students to Britain to study.

It is pointed out that a large proportion of the 4,000 applications for asylum to the U.K. processed each year are from students in colleges and universities.

Articles

Allison, Mary. "A Review of Proposals to Strengthen Foreign Language and International Education". *Foreign Language Annals* 19 (December, 1986): 533-536.

This review indicates a need for a strong federal role in terms of programs and grants for elementary, secondary, and post-secondary levels of study.

Anderson, Malcolm. "Overseas Students and British Foreign Policy". In *Readings in Overseas Student Policy*, eds. G. Williams, M. Kenyon and L. Williams (London: Overseas Students Trust, 1987): 33-46.

Overseas student questions enjoy only a low political salience in Britain. If this is to change, overseas student policy will have to be considered in the context of the general objectives of Britain's foreign policy, in particular her external cultural policy. The author contends that cultural exchange and cultural diplomacy worldwide are becoming increasingly important, but in Britain a number of factors have inhibited the development of an external cultural policy. The fact that major competitors like France, Germany, and Japan are all much more active and invest significantly more money in this area should be a source of concern to the British government. But in reality, the British overseas student policy is at best equivocal, resulting in the small investment of resources and in the absence of clear political direction. Although recent developments may give some grounds for cautious optimism, a coherent overseas student strategy remains a long way off.

Bacchus, M. K. "Towards a Strategy for Increasing Student Mobility Between Less Developed Countries in the Commonwealth Through Third Country Training". *International Journal of Educational Development* 6, No. 4 (1986): 275-285.

The articles discusses the policy of third-country training, i.e., the efforts by the economically more developed countries to provide through their aid programs the opportunity for students from the less developed countries to study at educational institutions outside the donor's country. It examines the current practices in this area of the major aid-granting Commonwealth countries -- Canada, Australia, New Zealand and Great Britain -- along with the advantages and limitations of such training. Suggestions are made for overcoming some of the problems that arise from efforts to implement this policy. Also discussed is what should be the nature and purpose of such institutions if one of their aims is to permit them to make a significant contribution to increasing our understanding of the problems of the less developed countries and further facilitating the flow of students between them.

Chishti, S. "International Demand for American Higher Education". *Research in Higher Education* 20, No. 3 (1984): 329-344.

An analysis of whether U.S. educational institutions should change policies concerning the increasing number of foreign students is presented. Statistical analyses are used to project enrollment into the 1980s. Factors leading to the rapid influx and likelihood of continuance are reviewed. It is concluded that there is little reason for concern.

Clarke, Michael. "Policy-Making on Overseas Students". In *Reading in Overseas Student Policy*, eds. G. Williams, M. Kenyon and L. Williams (London: Overseas Student Trust, 1987): 87-102.

The chapter contends that there is no properly articulated government policy on overseas students in Britain, but merely the components of one. The awareness of the overseas student issue has been heightened by the full-cost fees controversy. However, the overseas student issue is a hybrid one, lacking a natural political constituency because it falls between the realms of education, foreign and cultural policy, public expenditure, and overseas aid. The policy machinery is thus decentralized and fragmentary and is built not around ministerial policymaking but around efficient interdepartmental liaison. It is essentially reactive in nature and incapable of initiating policy change. The article concludes that, although the hybrid nature of the issue accounts for its present lack of political immediacy, it does not detract from its importance. There is nothing inevitable about the way in which the overseas student issue is not regarded as a significant policy issue in this country.

Courter, J. "Willing Hearts and Minds: Foreign Scholarship and Foreign Policy". *Policy Review* 33 (Summer, 1985): 74-76.

Fenwick, Keith. "Making the Most of Overseas Students". *Higher Education Quarterly* 41 (Spring, 1987): 126-137.

The present financial difficulties of higher education have put the educational case for overseas students back on the agenda. In this article, the author argues that the alternative and sometimes conflicting rhetorics of "internationalism" and "Third World modernization" have to be re-examined. The general case for overseas students stemming from liberal education principles can be supplemented by specification of a range of benefits they may bring. One condition of realizing these benefits is systematic thinking and positive action in the institution. Another, even more fundamental, condition is the integration of overseas student provision into an international education policy, and of that policy in the overall policy of the institution.

Fraser, Stewart E. "Australia and International Education: The Goldring and Jackson Reports -- Mutual Aid or Uncommon Advantage?" *Vestes* 27, No. 2 (1984): 15-29.

The article summarizes the results and implications of two major Australian foreign policy reports focusing on the role of foreign students in Australia's international educational exchanges and in regional economic aid and development programs. The two reports reflect different approaches (humanism vs. efficiency) to somewhat similar issues.

Fraser, Stewart E. "Overseas Students in Australia: Government Policies and Institutional Support". *Comparative Education Review* 28 (May, 1984): 279-299.

Describes the situation of overseas students in Australia in the recent 20 years and analyzes the government policy of both commonwealth and states concerning overseas students with the focus on recent years. Points out that overseas applicants will not be granted preference over Australian students in the contemporary political and educational climate and, as a result, the participation rate of overseas students will be lowered, with the increasing quota restrictions being imposed on them. Concludes that unless specific and selective funding is provided for the tertiary sector to cater to an increasing demand by both Australian and overseas students, these institutions will be forced on a priority basis to cater predominantly to the former to the detriment of the latter.

Hicks, Joseph E. "Foreign Student Policy in Japan: Getting Ready for the 21st Century". *Research in Higher Education (Daigaku Ronshu)* 14 (1985): 189-208.

Deals with the fundamental policy directions toward foreign students in Japan, stressing that a policy for overseas students in the 21st century should aim at admitting numbers of overseas students at an average rate of the present-day western countries, Japanese citizens should develop a spirit of internationalism. The government should actively take initiatives, and the Japanese universities should be made attractive to overseas students. Also discussed are two major policy concerns -- admission/placement and distribution; some differences in admissions procedures for MESC-sponsored, home-government-sponsored students and privately sponsored foreign students; and why and how distribution and allocation of foreign students should be implemented.

Kaplan, Robert B. "Foreign Students: Developing Institutional Policy". *College Board Review* No. 143 (Spring, 1987): 7-9 and 28-30.

Kida, Hiroshi. "A 100,000 Foreign Students Policy for Japan?" *Research in Higher Education (Daigaku Ronshu)* No. 15 (1986): 147-154.

Kobayashi, Tetsuya. "The Internationalization of Japanese Education". *Comparative Education* 22, No. 1 (1986): 65-71.

Describes the traditional Japanese attitude to international education. Reviews the efforts made by the government and concerned agencies to strengthen and improve international education. Identifies the factors preventing the progress of internationalization in the Japanese society in general and in the educational system in particular. Stresses that internationalization in education cannot be advanced by adding some novel educational policies while the existing educational system remains unchanged. Therefore, major changes in the existing system should take place.

THE BIBLIOGRAPHY

McDonald, Hamish. "Freeze on Foreigners: Canberra puts the lid on Overseas Student Enrollment". *Far Eastern Economic Review* (April 4, 1985): 1-12.

Smith, Alan. "Foreign Study in Western Europe: Policy Trends and Issues". In *Bridges to Knowledge -- Foreign Students in Comparative Perspective*, ed. E. Barber et al. (Chicago: University of Chicago Press, 1984): 115-129.

Identifies certain broad characteristics of the type of measures introduced by Western European countries, pointing out that common to most is a trend away from more open, indiscriminate policies toward more "regulatory" and "differentiated" approaches. Indicates patterns in national policies in these countries and analyzes the restrictiveness and differentiation in policies at the European level. Examines the creation of support schemes for the purpose of developing "organization mobility" programs, pointing out that they do appear to offer the most promising way forward and can contribute to the creation of favorable conditions for more generalized mobility. Concludes that the two approaches to the policy objective of promoting increased mobility among European countries and the stimulation of great "organized mobility" should be seen as an integrated dual approach comprising two mutually complementary elements.

Vaudiaux, Jacques. "Les politiques nationales d'acces des etudiants etrangers". *CRE-Information* 57 (1982): 7-24.

The president of the University of Dijon in France discusses the broader questions relating to foreign students in this article. He indicates some problems of defining foreign students and distinctions among students who may be refugees, children of migrant workers, and those in more common categories. The policies of the various host countries also differ, and this creates difficulties for the students. Access varies from country to country, with changes in policy difficult to follow in some cases. There is a particular concern with developing a common policy for the countries of the European Community as well as making special arrangements for students from the Third World.

Williams, Gareth. "The International Market for Overseas Students in the English-Speaking World". *European Journal of Education* 22, No. 1 (1987): 15-25.

The article presents an overview of the historical developments and current trends in the government policies concerning overseas students in Britain. It also gives an analysis of the effects of those policies, the responses of the universities and the public sector, and the educational, social, and economic considerations that went into overseas student policies.

Woodhall, Maureen. "Government Policy Towards Overseas Students: An International Perspective". *Higher Education Quarterly* 41 (Spring, 1987): 119-125.

Since the number of foreign students increased dramatically in the 1970s, several host countries became concerned over the rising cost of subsidizing students from abroad. Some countries, including Australia, Canada, and Britain, introduced differential fees for overseas students, while other countries use quotas to regulate or restrict foreign student numbers; still other countries, notably Japan, have tried to increase recruitment of foreign students. This paper compares recent enrollment trends and developments in government policy towards foreign students in ten countries (Australia, Belgium, Canada, France, West Germany, India, Japan, Russia, the United Kingdom, and the United States).

7. Economic Aspects: Cost-Benefit Analysis of "Sending" Countries

Books

Ghosh, B. N. and Ghosh, R. *Economics of Brain Migration*. New Delhi: Deep and Deep, 1982. 174 pp.

Articles

Blomquvist, Ake G. "International Migration of Educated Manpower and Social Rates of Return to Education in LDCs". *International Economic Review* 27, No. 1 (1986): 165-174.

Fry, Gerald. "The Economic and Political Impact of Study Abroad". *Comparative Education Review* 28 (May, 1984): 203-220.

> The article analyzes the impact of study abroad in the developed countries. It identifies possible positive effects of study abroad in terms of political development; development of technical skills, foreign language competency, regional consciousness, and greater sensitivity to the need for cultural democracy; international economic effects and foreign exchange remittances and enhancement of mobility opportunities through study abroad; and cross-cultural enrichment effects. Some possible negative effects of study abroad include foreign exchange costs, individual opportunity costs, socialization into a consumer culture, incorporation into the structure of the dominating center, and the problem of cultural marginality. The article concludes that the investment in supporting study abroad for individuals from developing countries has been well justified, and that it is discouraging that the funding for cross-cultural study abroad is becoming more and more difficult while global spending on military armaments continues to spiral. It emphasizes that study abroad has positive economic and political effects over the long term and is a basic building block in the development of a peaceful, cooperative global community.

Ghosh, B. N. "Brain Migration from the Third World: An Implicative Analysis". *Rivista Internazionale di Scienze economiche e commerciali* 31 (April, 1984): 346-370.

This study analyzes the implications of brain migration from the viewpoints of less developed countries. It critically examines the views expressed by nationalists and internationalists in this context. The implications of brain exchange and brain export are found to be beneficial types of brain migration, brain drain involves a loss of strategically important manpower, slowing down the tempo of development and creation of large external diseconomies. Brain overflow, for a thickly populated LDC, can act as a safety valve to release the surplus manpower and thereby to minimize educated unemployment problem. Brain drain is wooed away without paying any compensation. Brain drain is, in fact, a form of reserve transfer of technology.

Lee, Kiong Hock and Tan, J. P. "The International Flow of Third Level Lesser Developed Country Students to Developed Countries: Determinants and Implications". *Higher Education* 13 (December, 1984): 687-708.

This study analyzes the international flow of third-level developing-country students to advanced countries from the perspective of sending authorities in developing countries. The magnitude of this flow can hardly be overemphasized; on the basis of a conservative estimate made in this article, the annual loss of foreign exchange entailed by this flow amounted to 17 percent of the interest repayment on total external debts of the lesser developed countries (LDCs) in 1979, a sum that the developing countries themselves can hardly ignore. On an aggregate basis, the principal hypothesis is that the outflow of students is determined by excess demand for third-level education in developing countries. The empirical results support this hypothesis, while pointing to the importance of other factors. Excess demand for third-level education in the developing countries is one of the most important determinants of the flow of developing-country students to the advanced nations. On the whole, expansion of developing-country tertiary education, at the national or regional levels, could effectively divert some of the flow to local institutions. Further, given the willingness and ability of the students to pay, as witnessed by the fact that the vast majority of developing-country students privately finance their education abroad, the expansion of third-level education in LDCs could be funded substantially by user charges and student-loan schemes.

8. Economic Aspects: Cost-Benefit Analysis of "Host" Countries

Books

Dresch, Stephen P. *The Economics of Foreign Students.* New York: Institute of International Education, 1987. 21 p.

> This essay focuses on the complex issue of the economic costs and benefits of foreign students in the context of American higher education. The stress is on the cost to institutions of higher education and to funding agencies rather than to individual students or to the sending countries. It is argued that it is very difficult to fix specific costs for foreign students, since the circumstances of enrollment vary dramatically. The addition of a student in a field that does not have a high demand, for example, is low. Further, foreign students provide important services in terms of teaching and research assistance in many universities and they provide enrollments in some fields that have a low demand at present. It is argued that foreign students provide a stabilization to the American higher education system and that their marginal costs are, in most fields, relatively low.

Solmon, Lewis, C. and Beddow, Ruth. *Flows, Costs, and Benefits of Foreign Students to the United States: Do We Have a Problem?* New York: Institute of International Education, 1984.

Throsby, C. D. *Economic Aspects of the Foreign Student Question, Economic Review*. Melbourne: Melbourne Press, 1986.

Williams, Gareth; Kenyon, Martin, and Williams, Lynn, eds. *Readings in Overseas Student Policy*. London: Overseas Students Trust, 1987. 142 p.

With the imposition of the "full fee" policy in Britain that imposed on foreign students the full cost of their education, foreign students became an issue of considerable debate. The numbers of foreign students declined by 36% between 1979, when the policy was imposed, and 1984. A number of scholarship schemes were set up to ease the burden on some students from targeted countries and in special categories (such as refugees). It is interesting that the declines in student numbers was greatest among students from the Commonwealth and the poorest countries, precisely the opposite of government intentions. This volume provides a series of data-based and informative essays on foreign student policy and on the impact of the post-1979 changes. Maureen Woodhall has written on an international perspective on government policy regarding foreign students, Malcolm Anderson on British foreign policy and foreign students, Michael Clarke on the process of policymaking in Britain regarding overseas students, Robin Marris on the commercial implications of foreign student policy, and Kenneth King on technical assistance and the role of overseas students.

Articles

Agarwal, Vinod B. and Winkler, Donald R. "United States Immigration Policy and Indirect Immigration of Professionals". *Economics of Education Review* 4, No. 1 (1985): 1-16.

Professionals migrate to the U.S. from other countries through direct and indirect channels. The indirect channel, which entails entering the U.S. as a foreign student or visitor and subsequently adjusting visa status to immigrant, has assumed increasing importance over time. The number of adjustments of status can be expected to further increase in the future as the eligible pool, comprised mainly of foreign students, continues to expand. The ratio of adjustments to the eligible pool is also influenced by U.S. immigration policy, which originates in administrative regulations as well as legislative action. U.S. immigration policy affects the ease of immigration and thus the ratio of adjustments to the eligible pool. Variations in immigration policy across countries and over time are found to have statistically significant impacts on this ratio.

Birch, Derek. "A Further Note on Costs and Student Fees (Developing a Policy for Recruiting Overseas Students)". *Coombe Lodge Report* 17, No. 12 (1985): 695-699.

Blum, Albert A. "Countertrading Textiles for Tuitions: A Way to Secure More Foreign Students". *Economics of Education Review* 6, No. 3 (1987): 307-309.

Chishti, S. "Economic Costs and Benefits of Educating Foreign Students in the United States". *Research in Higher Education* 21, No. 4 (1984): 397-414.

In recent years some western European countries have adopted restrictive rationing/pricing policies to regulate the accelerated inflow of foreign students. There is no such policy in the U.S. If the current trends continue, the population of foreign students in the U.S. may reach one million by 1990. In view of their large and rapidly expanding number, it is of some interest to study the economics of their education. An attempt is made here to estimate the economic costs and economic benefits to the U.S. of educating foreign students. It should be emphasized at the outset that the conceptual and data problems have made it impossible to estimate some economic costs and benefits, thereby constraining the comprehensiveness of the overall estimates.

Fielden, John and Dalrymple, Hew. "Flexibility in Setting Fees". In *Readings in Overseas Student Policy*, eds. G. Williams, M. Kenyon, and L. Williams (London: Overseas Students Trust, 1987): 115-120.

The chapter considers the various issues relating to the fees that are charged to overseas students. The introduction of "full-cost" fees by the British government in 1980 had a dramatic effect on the overseas student intake initially. Since that date, there has been a steady, slow recovery in numbers. Against this background, the authors consider three topics: experience so far in setting fees, the alternative approaches that are available, and the theoretical and practical implications of each.

Hardern, G. S. "A Note on Marginal Costing and Student Fees, (Developing a Policy for Reuniting Overseas Students: Part 2)". *Coombe Lodge Report* 17, No. 12 (1985): 692-694.

Mace, John. "Overseas Student Fee Policy: Some Economic Considerations". *Higher Education Review* 19 (Summer, 1987): 37-54.

In November 1979, the British government announced that overseas students in British higher education would, from October 1980, be charged "full-cost" fees. Is this policy sound economically or otherwise? This article lays out some of the theoretical considerations that should inform the government policy towards overseas students' fees and then makes a rough estimate of the costs and benefits of overseas students studying in the United Kingdom. The calculations show a net gain to the British taxpayer from having overseas students in British universities and a substantial gain for overseas students in non-advanced further education. Although the article is confined to a narrow cost-benefit analysis ignoring the political, social and educational costs and benefits of recruiting overseas students, the author believes that these less easily quantifiable costs and benefits may in aggregate be more important than those analyzed within the narrow cost-benefit framework. The author concludes that the overseas student fee is too high and unless the government can justify it on sound economic (and non-economic) grounds, foreign governments, overseas students, and British educationalists will continue to believe that the present policy is based on prejudice, ignorance, and bigotry.

Marris, Robin. "Assessing the Commercial Element in Overseas Student Policy". In *Readings in Overseas Student Policy*, eds. G. Williams, M. Kenyon, and L. Williams (London: Overseas Students Trust, 1987): 71-85.

> The concept of commercial benefits to Britain from overseas students is founded in the belief that bringing overseas students to the country is a particularly effective form of export promotion. The article argues that there is a strong case for publicly financed promotion of exports because they stimulate economic growth and employment. The long-term commercial impact of overseas students is not precisely quantifiable, but one should not therefore automatically assume that it is small, as policymakers seem to do at present. By conducting an econometric "thought experiment", the author illustrates that the potential benefits in terms of the future volume of exports might equally well be very large and concludes that subsidizing overseas students can be highly profitable activity.

Niven, Alastair. "Salad Days Without the Dressing? What British Higher Education and Further Education Can Do for Their Overseas Students". *Higher Education Quarterly* 41 (Spring, 1987): 144-161.

> The introduction of "full-cost" fees by the government in 1980 had a dramatic effect on the overseas student intake initially. But since then there has been a steady, slow recovery in numbers. This paper considers three issues relating to the fees that are charged to overseas students: experiences so far in setting fees, the alternative approaches that are available, and the theoretical and practical implications of each.

Rogers, Kenneth. "Foreign Students: Economic Benefit or Liability?". *College Board Review* No. 133 (Fall, 1984): 20-25.

> The author argues that the economic benefits of enrolling foreign students in colleges and universities far outweigh the liabilities. Therefore, foreign-student enrollment should be studied,

developed, justified, and improved like any other U.S. industry that hopes to retain its competitive edge in world trade.

Throsby, C. D. "Cost Functions for Australian Universities". *Australian Economic Papers* 25 (December, 1986): 175-192.

Throsby, C. D. "Economic Aspects of the Foreign Student Question". *Economic Record* 62 (1986): 400-414.

> Foreign students comprise about 4% of total student enrollment in the tertiary-education sector in Australia. The numbers of private overseas students in Australia are regulated by quota and by the imposition of a subsidized fee. Australian government policy towards overseas students has been discussed in two recent government reports that reach conflicting conclusions about desirable policy changes. In this paper, Throsby puts forward the arguments against which the economic aspects of these two reports can be judged, discussing the theoretical basis for regulation by fees and quotas and applying these considerations in the present Australian context. He finds that, despite some recent moves in the right direction, Australian policy towards foreign students and towards the use of tertiary education as a medium of foreign aid is still short of ideal when judged on economic grounds.

Totimeh, E. C. and Harris, G. T. "Expected Rates of Return to Overseas Student Postgraduate Study in Australia". *Vestes* 27, No. 1 (1984): 38-41.

> A study comparing the expected increased life earnings with the educational and other costs of foreign graduate students studying in Australia suggests that in addition to the estimated social benefits, the private benefits to students indicate that the financial aid awarded them is a worthwhile investment.

Wilce, H. "British Setback in the Battle for Brains". *Far Eastern Economic Review* 129 (August 22, 1985): 88-89.

Williams, Peter. "Britain's Full-Cost Policy for Overseas Students". *Comparative Education Review* 28 (May, 1984): 258-278.

Discusses the issues raised by the full-cost fees policy for overseas students imposed by the British government: issues of cost calculation in higher education, of dual pricing policies, of the place of a private enclave in a public system, of accountability and shifts in accountability when the price to the consumer of a service is steeply raised. Finds that the effects of the full-cost fees policy in Britain have been less clear-cut and dramatic than many people anticipated, and that the damage to college and university physical and financial viability has been half obscured by attacks on the financial base of postsecondary education on a broader front than overseas students and by the crisis of domestic provision as home numbers reach their peak. Concludes that the longer-term issues will not go away and the overseas student question is likely to remain as important domestically as it is internationally.

Winkler, Donald R. "The Costs and Benefits of Foreign Students in United States Higher Education". *Journal of Public Policy* 4 (May, 1984): 115-138.

This paper makes a twofold contribution to the practical application of cost-benefit analysis and to our understanding of the costs and benefits to the host country of foreign students in higher education. First, within the technical constraints it develops a model for assessing costs and benefits; this model is potentially applicable to all countries with foreign students. The model includes educational and political as well as economic inputs, and the paper discusses qualitative as well as quantitative costs and benefits. Secondly, the model is applied to the particular case of the United States. The significance of different perspectives for assessing net benefit is recognized, and costs and benefits are assessed from the perspectives of higher education institutions, state residents, and all U.S. citizens. The paper finds positive net benefits, subject to a number of assumptions. However, the policies of both state governments and the U.S. government do not appear to be consistent with the goal of maximizing this net benefit.

Woodhall, Maureen. "Financing Student Flows: The Effects of Recent Policy Trends". *Economics of Education Review* 6, No. 2 (1987): 195-204.

During 1970-80, total foreign student enrollment nearly doubled, from 500,000 to over 900,000. The growth of foreign study has led several countries to introduce quotas or differential fees to regulate or restrict foreign student enrollments. This paper examines recent policy developments in host countries and draws on a survey of foreign students in Britain in 1985. An analysis of the effects of full-cost fees, introduced in Britain in 1980, shows that this caused a reduction in the number of students, especially from developing countries, but since 1983 a policy of targeted scholarships has helped to redress the balance. The general tendency in the main host countries in recent years has been towards a greater awareness of the importance of foreign students, and also a shift towards policies designed to regulate foreign student flows. The shift towards cost recovery and selective student support has succeeded in concentrating scarce resources on students from particular regions. This trend is likely to lead to further reassessment by sending countries of their policies towards student flows. Governments are paying more attention to the question of who benefits from these subsidies and developing new policies to ensure that both sending and receiving countries benefit from increased student mobility.

9. Overseas Study and Socioeconomic Development

Books

British Council. Committee for International Cooperation on Higher Education. *The British Ph.D. and the Overseas Student.* London: The British Council, 1984.

Heaney, Linda. *Education for International Development: Building a Constituency -- A Report of a Seminar.* Washington, D.C.: National Association for Foreign Student Affairs, 1986. 12 p.

A report based on the participants' contributions at the seminar on "Education for International Development: Building a Constituency", this volume assesses current realities, issues, and tensions in U.S. public and private-sector involvement in development education. It identifies several successful development education efforts and recommends actions that participants can take to communicate the importance of development assistance to the American public whose support is critical for effective international activities.

Articles

Gao, Weizhen. "The Open Door and the Reform of Higher Education". *Chinese Education* 21 (Spring, 1988): 116-128.

Hawkins, J. N. "Educational Exchanges and the Transformation of Higher Education in the People's Republic of China". In *Bridges to Knowledge -- Foreign Students in Comparative Perspective*, eds. E. Barber, P. Altbach and R. Myers (Chicago: University of Chicago Press, 1984): 19-31.

A study of scholars from the People's Republic of China who had studied in the United States in the past decade and who returned to China. These scholars expressed great interest in the nature of

American higher education and in the possibility of implementing American-style reforms in Chinese higher education. They expressed interest in faculty relations, research, curriculum, and teaching, among other things.

Hua, Xue. "New Blood on the Qinghua Campus: A Report on Qinghua Scholars Who Have Returned from Abroad". *Chinese Education* 21 (Spring, 1988): 73-81.

Moock, Joyce Lewinger. "Overseas Training and National Development Objectives in Sub-Saharan Africa". *Comparative Education Review* 28 (May, 1984): 221-240.

Discusses the impact of overseas training on national development objectives in sub-Saharan Africa. Reviews the current economic crisis in Africa and the needs for high-level manpower possessing particular development-oriented skills. Examines the pros and cons of foreign study as one alternative for meeting national training requirements for competent indigenous professionals. Points out areas where more systematic information is needed about the impact associated with training in foreign countries and suggests some conditions related to the effective provision of overseas education.

Myers, Robert G. "Foreign Training and Development Strategies". In *Bridges to Knowledge -- Foreign Students in Comparative Perspective*, ed. E. Barber et al. (Chicago: University of Chicago Press, 1984): 147-63.

Focuses on the externally financed study abroad at the post-graduate level from 1960 to 1980. Compares two main strategies: institution-building strategy and discipline-building strategy. Examines support for foreign study provided by the Ford Foundation in Peru, with special attention to effects of a changing economic and political climate on policy and outcomes. Points to the risks associated with a narrow institution-building strategy as a guide to support for study abroad. Suggests that a small continuing investment in foreign training can have an important impact on the growth of a discipline. Reinforces the position that brain drain associated with external support for training abroad is not large and is not a very important issue.

Radhakrishna, S. "Postgraduate Courses -- Impact in Developing Countries". *Higher Education in Europe* 11, No. 4 (1986): 27-30.

Umakoshi, Toru and Park, Yung H. "The Role of Overseas Education for National Development of the Republic of Korea: 1953-1972". *Research in Higher Education (Daigaku Ronshu)* 14 (1985): 169-188.

The article discusses a number of questions related to foreign education and Korea's elite training, including the significance of foreign education to elite training, the specific roles foreign education performs, and the specific contributions developed nations (mainly the United States and Japan) have made toward elite training in Korea. It is found that Japan and the U.S. have played a significant role in educating South Korea's elite and that the foreign-trained elite have performed a vital role in implementing the country's development plans. A close relationship between the requirements of the development plans and the areas of specialization chosen by R.O.K. students studying abroad is also noted.

10. Legal Issues

Books

National Association for Foreign Student Affairs. *Plan of Implementation for a New System of Students/Schools Regulations Governing Nonimmigrant Students.* Washington, D.C.: National Association for Foreign Student Affairs, 1985.

Smith, Eugene H. and Baron, Marvin J. *Faculty Member's Guide to U.S. Immigration Law.* Washington, D.C.: National Association of Foreign Student Affairs, 1986. 47 p.

This brief summary of the complexities of the new United States immigration law is aimed at college and university faculty members. It is a "must" for anyone concerned with foreign students, since it provides a clear and concise summary of a highly complex issue -- immigration regulations. Specialists will, of course, need more detailed information, but this booklet provides basic information and interpretation for the non-specialist. It defines immigration categories, working regulations, and the like. It is written clearly and reflects the current (1986) regulations.

Articles

Weston, Julia. "Visa Students Facing 'Multiplicity of Problems'". *University Affairs* 27 (February, 1986): 2-3.

11. Recruitment: Policies and Procedures

Books

National Liaison Committee on Foreign Student Admissions, and National Association for Foreign Student Affairs. *Recruitment Kit: An Introduction to Foreign Student Recruitment.* Washington, D.C.: National Association for Foreign Student Affairs, 1985.

Responsible Recruitment: A Model for a Code of Practice. London: United Kingdom Council for Overseas Student Affairs.

A brief set of guidelines for recruitment of overseas students aimed mainly at British academic institutions involved in recruiting students abroad. The issue of overseas student recruitment has been a key topic in Britain, as there have been problems with inappropriate recruitment practices.

Zikopoulos, Marianthi and Barber, Eleanor G. *Choosing Schools from Afar: The Selection of Colleges and Universities in the United States by Foreign Students*. New York: Institute of International Education, 1986. 59 p.

This study looks at how foreign students in the United States select the institutions that they attend. Among the findings are:

1. 75% of the respondents are satisfied with the institutions they selected. In most important respects, the schools meet their expectations.

2. About 30% of the respondents find that the costs of attending university are higher than they expected and that they are somewhat disappointed with their relationships with their professors, the community, and with the recreational opportunities available to them.

3. The principal attraction of foreign study in the U.S. is the perceived high quality of education.

4. Most foreign students utilize the brochures and catalogs of American universities that they are able to find in their home countries. They also frequently obtain information from friends, relatives, and government and private information agencies. Respondents consider the main information sources they use as reliable.

Articles

"Developing a Policy for Recruiting Overseas Students: Part 1". *Coombe Lodge Report* 17, No. 12 (1985): 664-685.

Stemming from current debates in Britain concerning recruitment of overseas students and edited by the U.K. Council on Overseas Student Affairs, this issue deals with a range of topics relating to the recruitment of overseas students. It is pointed out that with the imposition of the full-fee policy, many academic institutions have had to be more aggressive in recruiting overseas students and that serious problems have arisen in recruitment practices. Articles consider such topics as the responsibilities of academic institutions in recruiting, factors to consider before embarking on overseas recruiting activities, and the like. Several articles considering the recruiting issue from the perspective of overseas students themselves are also included.

"Developing a Policy for Recruiting Overseas Students: Part II". *Coombe Lodge Report* 17, No. 12 (1985): 686-712.

The second special issue devoted to British concerns about recruiting foreign students deals with such topics as admissions issues for foreign students, developing a marketing strategy for recruiting overseas, the costs of recruiting and educating foreign students in general, and related items. Considerable attention is paid to the economic factors of foreign study from the viewpoint of British academic institutions.

Ecclesfield, Nigel. "Responsibility in Recruitment: The Institution and Its Policy". *Coombe Lodge Report* 17, No. 11 (1985): 618-626.

Raises some of the issues involved in the way in which institutions handle the problem of overseas students and argues that institutions ought to have a clearly defined policy as the cornerstone of their recruitment effort. Points out that a coherent institutional policy for overseas students would not only benefit overseas students, but also serve to focus attention on areas where improvements would benefit other students and staff. Puts forward some recommendations concerning policies for overseas student recruitment and believes that the only way by which all these recommendations can be implemented is to have an institutional policy firmly committed to multi-cultural anti-racist education.

"Issues for Institutions to Address Before Embarking on Recruitment and Contracting: Questions Asked and Conclusions Reached by Conference Working Groups, (Developing a Policy for Recruiting Overseas Students: Part 1)". *Coombe Lodge Report* 17, No. 11 (1985): 627-637.

"The Needs and Expectations of Overseas Students: Issues and Conclusions Reached by Working Groups During the Conference (Developing a Policy for Recruiting Overseas Students: Part 1)". *Coombe Lodge Report* 17, No. 11 (1985): 644-654.

Rowland, Keith. "Contracting Overseas Students: The Issues, (Developing a Policy for Recruiting Overseas Students: Part 2)". *Coombe Lodge Report* 17, No. 12 (1985): 671-678.

Thachaberry, Mark D. and Liston, Antoinette. "Recruitment and Admissions: Special Issues and Ethical Considerations". In *Guiding the Development of Foreign Students*, ed. K. Pyle (San Francisco, London: Jossey-Bass, 1986): 29-38.

> Discusses the recruitment and admission of foreign students. Provides an overview of the factors and pressures surrounding these processes. Pays special attention to matters of ethics that need to be attended to as pressure grows on admissions offices to recruit foreign students. Provides guidelines to assist admissions offices and student affairs divisions to establish policies in this area. Stresses that the salient factor of an ethical recruitment program is the honest and accurate presentation of information to the prospective student.

12. Admissions: Policies and Procedures

Books

Del Barrio, Fidel. *A Study of Foreign Student Enrollments and Admission Policies at Texas Public Community/Junior Colleges*. Ed.D. Dissertation, East Texas State University, 1986. 63 p. Order No. DA8614723

Findings. School size, type, and location did not significantly influence foreign-student-enrollment rates for the forty-seven colleges as a whole. Two of the three border colleges were high with respect to foreign-student-enrollment rates but required no English proficiency test, no set criteria for inspection of academic background, and no posting of bonds or deposits.

Conclusions. Whether a college was small or large, rural or urban, or did or did not apply any of the thirteen major admission criteria had no significant relationship to the foreign-student-enrollment rates for the forty-seven colleges. These enrollments rose steadily during the 1970s, peaked around 1980 at about 2% of all enrollment in the TPCJCs, declined, and then leveled off at about 1.5% during the 1981-83 period. Increasing standards for the Test of English As a Foreign Language (raised to 550 by some schools), higher proficiency requirements for English As a Second Language, higher grade-point averages, and closer inspection of academic and other credentials of foreign students by certain individual college districts contributed toward lowering foreign-student enrollment, especially during the 1981-83 period. Social/political factors, the Middle East crisis, political and economic conditions in foreign countries, Iranian students sent home, lack of acceptance by fellow students and townspeople, tighter immigration regulations, peso devaluation, and the United States government's discouragement of foreign students attending American schools tended to decrease foreign-student-enrollment rates.

Johnson, J. K., ed. *The Admission and Academic Placement of Students from Bahrain, Oman, Qatar, United Arab Emirates, Yemen Arab Republic.* Washington, D.C.: National Association for Foreign Student Affairs, 1984.

In order to assist U.S. colleges and universities as they work with international student agencies and representatives from Bahrain, Oman, Qatar, the United Arab Emirates, and the Yemen Arab Republic, this volume provides relevant information on these countries' educational systems and offers placement recommendations for each of them. The country profiles cover the country and its people, the educational system, pre-primary and primary education, intermediate and secondary education, public and private secondary-school courses, secondary vocational-training programs, military schools, technical and industrial education, agricultural education, higher education, teacher education, and English language training. Also provided are sample documents from these countries, including transcripts and diplomas, bibliographies, and a glossary.

Packwood, Virginia M. and Packwood, William T. *Admission Requirements for International Students at Colleges and Universities in the United States.* Fargo, ND: Two Trees Press, 1986.

Undergraduate and graduate admissions requirements for foreign students at more than 2,000 U.S. colleges and universities are detailed in this handbook. Based on responses to questionnaires sent to all U.S. higher education institutions, the context emphasizes minimum scores required on the TOEFL, possible alternative qualifications, required GPA, and the existence of an intensive English program. It also includes such standard information as school location, type (private, public, undergraduate and graduate), foreign student enrollment, application deadlines, and telephone numbers for contact. This guide is designed to supplement other sources of information on U.S. institutions and to help students make better, informed decisions about schools where they might most successfully be considered for admission.

Sarich, Safija. *The Relationship of Secondary School Achievement to International Student Success at a Private United States University.* Unpublished Ed.D. Dissertation, United States International University, 1985. 175 p. Order No. DA8517823

This study tested the accuracy of the admission average in predicting the academic success of international students at an American university. The admission average was based on either results of subjects examinations taken upon completion of secondary school or grades assigned by teachers at the end of each school term (depending upon the type of assessment submitted by the student). A goal of the study was to determine whether one type of assessment of secondary school achievement was a better predictor than was the other.

Articles

Gross, Virginia and Althen, Gary. "Obstacles to Foreign Admissions Research: A Case Study". *College and University* 61 (Winter, 1986): 128-134.

A study of predictors of academic success among Nigerian students in two U.S. universities encountered the problem of too small a sample despite methodological precautions. It raised the question of whether it is possible to establish general placement recommendations applicable to foreign students in different institutions and from different countries.

Hecker, Jo Ann K. "On Refining the Ritual of Assessing the Foreign Graduate Applicant". *College and University* 59 (Summer, 1984): 334-337.

American graduate schools need to sharpen their techniques when screening the growing group of foreign applicants requiring professional skills. An institution's admissions process can either enhance its overall institutional quality and prestige or seriously harm it in a short time.

Lancashire, Frank. "Admission of Overseas Students: An LEA Perspective (Developing a Policy for Recruiting Overseas Students: Part 2)". *Coombe Lodge Report* 17, No. 12 (1985): 665-670.

Slocum, Joel. "Trends and Prospects in Foreign Student Admissions". *College Board Review* No. 132 (Summer, 1984): 23-25, 33.

The availability of financial aid is one of the most important factors affecting the choices of many foreign students for study in the United States, whereas availability of places and the competition for them vary. Access to undergraduate engineering programs is seen as almost impossible.

13. Evaluation of Credentials and Equivalence of Degrees

Books

Krawutschke, Eleanor and Roberts, Thomas, eds. *Transcripts from Study Abroad Programs -- A Workbook*. Washington, D.C.: National Association for Foreign Student Affairs, 1986. 59 p.

Porter, Georgeanne B. *Federal Republic of Germany. A Study of the Educational System of the Federal Republic of Germany and a Guide to the Academic Placement of Students in Educational Institutions of the United States. World Education Series.* Washington, D.C.: American Association of Collegiate Registrars and Admissions Officers, 1986. 196 p.

Schuler, Peter. *The Netherlands: A Study of the Educational System of the Netherlands and a Guide to the Academic Placement of Students in Educational Institutions of the United States. World Education Series.* Washington, D.C.: American Association of Collegiate Registrars and Admissions Officers, 1984.

The discussion on the educational system of the Netherlands covers the legal and financial bases of Dutch education and the various educational levels and types of schooling, such as preprimary, primary and special education; secondary education; higher vocational education; teacher education; nursing education; university education; and international education. Guidelines are included on stratification in Dutch education, Dutch credentials, examinations and grading practices, and conversion to U.S. units of credit. Placement recommendations are provided for each level/type of schooling.

Simmons, Ruth J. *Haiti: A Study of the Educational System of Haiti and a Guide to the Academic Placement of Students in Educational Institutions of the United States. World Education Series.* Washington, D.C.: American Association of Collegiate Registrars and Admissions Officers, 1985. 132 p.

The description of Haiti's educational system covers primary and secondary education, vocational training at the secondary level, teacher training, the State University of Haiti, university centers, and non-university tertiary-level training. Information is included on Haitian degrees, certificates, and diplomas. Placement recommendations approved by the National Council on the Evaluation of Foreign Educational Credentials are also provided. For each type of credential, information is provided on the entrance requirements, length of study, study programs that the credential is a prerequisite for in Haiti, and the placement recommendation for study in the United States.

Sjogren, Clifford F. and Kerr, Lornie G. *Norway: A Guide to the Admission and Academic Placement of Norwegian Students in North American Colleges and Universities.* Washington, D.C.: National Association for Foreign Student Affairs/College Board, 1985. 104 p.

As part of the Projects for International Education Research, this volume provides information on Norwegian education and recommendations for admissions and academic placement of Norwegian students in U.S. colleges and universities. The overview of Norwegian education includes information on the structure of the system, course descriptions, grading, examinations, certificates and degrees, and faculty. The role of the National Council on the Evaluation of Foreign Educational Credentials is also considered. In addition, the volume provides placement recommendations and information for 49 kinds of educational credentials, including information on program entrance eligibility requirements and the length of the programs.

Stedman, Joann Bye. *Malaysia: A Study of the Educational System of Malaysia and a Guide to the Academic Placement of Students in*

Educational Institutions of the United States. Washington, D.C.: American Association of Collegiate Registrars and Admissions Officers, 1986. 188 p.

Wellington, Stanley. *Colombia: A Study of the Educational System of Colombia and a Guide to the Academic Placement of Students from Colombia in Educational Institutions of the United States. World Education Series.* Washington, D.C.: American Association of Collegiate Registrars and Admissions Officers, 1984.

> The discussion on educational system of Colombia covers a description of different levels of schooling; the pre-1974 and current secondary-school curricula and grading systems, and undergraduate admissions, credits, transfer practices, examinations, degrees, and diplomas. The following levels of college studies are examined: intermediate professional studies, technological studies, university studies, specialist programs, master's programs, and doctoral programs. Guidelines and placement recommendations are presented as they pertain to Colombian degrees and diplomas, military and police training, and transfer of credits from Colombian institutions.

Articles

Dalichow, Fritz. "Academic Recognition Within the European Community". *European Journal of Education* 22, No. 1 (1987): 39-58.

> Student mobility is deficient within the member states of the European Community, in part because academic recognition of higher education entrance qualifications, study periods, intermediate and final examinations is not automatic between EC countries. Mutual trust and confidence in the quality of higher education within other member states is lacking. In this article, the author demonstrates how things have moved and are moving in the field of academic recognition within the community. He also argues that academic recognition is not an isolated issue, but is embedded in the larger fields of higher education cooperation and education cooperation.

Deloz, M. "The Activities of the Council of Europe Concerning the Recognition of Studies and Diplomas of Higher Education and of Academic Mobility". *Higher Education in Europe* 11, No. 1 (1986): 21-27.

This article provides a survey of the initiatives taken and the activities carried out by the Council of Europe with regard to the recognition of higher education studies and diplomas, and with regard to academic mobility. The objectives of the council are to ensure and encourage co-operation among European nations in the area of higher education and university research and to promote relations among universities and institutions of higher education and research. Some of the obstacles identified in the attempt to attain the objectives include organization and dissemination of information, academic and administrative prerequisites to mobility, problems posed by foreign students in the receiving countries, linguistic problems, and financial support.

Hagen, Jon. "University Co-operation and Academic Recognition in Europe: The Council of Europe and the Communities". *European Journal of Education* 22, No. 1 (1987): 77-83.

The article presents an overview of the means employed by the European communities and the Council of Europe in the field of academic mobility and recognition of qualifications and diplomas intended to promote interchange and cooperation in higher education. Juxtaposing developments and initiatives supported by the EC and the Council of Europe may illustrate a seemingly increasing divergence between the opportunities available to institutions, staff, and students in higher education in the countries within and without the EC. As Hagen argues, if developments occur in the direction of a growing disparity in the degree of involvement of European countries in their efforts towards international academic cooperation, undesirable effects on the pattern of European student and staff mobility could result.

Jablonska-Skinder, Hanna. "Bringing the Convention of Prague to Life: The Case of Poland". *European Journal of Education* 22, No. 1 (1987): 59-76.

> The article outlines the nature and implementation of the underlying principles of the convention signed by 10 socialist countries in Prague on June 7, 1972, that related to the mutual recognition of the equivalence of both general and professional secondary-school leaving certificates, as well as final diplomas awarded by higher institutions. Though it mainly focuses on Poland, references are made where appropriate to other socialist countries. Having analyzed the problems and difficulties in implementing the principles of the Prague Convention, the author expresses the hope that the activities of the (European) Regional Committee of UNESCO and others will contribute to further steady progress in this field.

Kalela, A. "Progress in Co-operation for the Implementation of the European Convention on the Recognition of Studies, Diplomas, and Degrees Concerning Higher Education". *Higher Education in Europe* 11, No. 1 (1986): 6-10.

> This article provides an analysis of the Convention on the Recognition of Studies, Diplomas, and Degrees concerning Higher Education in Europe that was adopted in 1979 under the auspices of UNESCO and is comprised of 21 states. The article reviews the status, the basic elements of the convention, and the major progress of cooperation between the European higher education systems. The article also focuses on the opportunity for exchange of information provided by the convention.

Popivoda-Endresen, N. "The Relevance for Developing Countries of International Mobility and the Recognition of Studies and Degrees of Higher Education". *Higher Education in Europe* 11, No. 3 (1986): 13-15.

> More than half of the foreign students enrolled in European higher education institutions are from developing countries. While this trend reflects on the vitality of the cooperation

between European and developing countries, there is evidence of competing trends. On the one hand, developing countries are demanding an increasing number of places in European universities, greater flexibility in the conditions of access, and guarantees that graduates return to their home countries. On the other hand, however, European countries are insisting on higher standards for access to higher education, and immigration laws are becoming more restrictive.

Razzano, A. "Conditions of Academic Mobility". *Universitas -- Studie documentazione di vita universitaria* 5, No. 14 (October-December, 1984): 39-45.

Van Dijk, Hans. "The Study Assessment Division of the Netherlands Universities Foundation for International Cooperation (VISUM/NEIC)". *Higher Education in Europe* 10, No. 2 (April-June, 1985): 118-121.

Discusses the role and functions of the Netherlands' interuniversity agency. Makes recommendations to Dutch organizations concerning the equivalency of education received abroad, stimulates international academic mobility, and provides information to Dutch nationals going abroad or potential foreign students in the Netherlands about Dutch higher education.

14. Finances: Sources and Problems

Books

U.S. General Accounting Office. *U.S. and Soviet Bloc Training of Latin American and Caribbean Students: Considerations in Developing Future U.S. Programs. (Report to the President of the Senate and the Speaker of the House).* Washington, D.C.: U.S. General Accounting Office (Report No. GAO/NSIAD-84-109), 1984.

Working Party on Crisis and Hardship Arrangements for Overseas Students. *Containing Crisis: The Response to Overseas Student Groups in Hardship.* London: United Kingdom Council of Overseas Student Affairs, 1985. 40 p.

> This is a unique document that focuses on the problems foreign students have when funds are disrupted or other unforseen difficulties occur. It is based on a British study. The stress in this report is on financial problems; it is strongly advised that institutions try to ensure that students will have sufficient funds prior to their arrival so that crises do not occur. When problems do occur, it is important to have adequate liaison with all relevant agencies, such as embassies, universities, and government agencies. Models for appropriate planning and crisis management are also provided. While the information in this report is related to Britain, the general perspective will be relevant for an American audience.

Articles

Durojaiye, S. M. and Donald, G. A. H. "Finance for Mature Overseas Students and Their Families". *Higher Education Review* 16 (Spring, 1984): 7-16.

> Results of a study of adult foreign students at the University College at Cardiff, Wales, indicate that most have financial responsibility for children and adults, often other than their own immediate families. Home-government support appears to be more readily available to male than female students, and most students are concerned about their financial resources.

Naff, Clayton. "University of Pennsylvania's Solution to Foreign Student Payment Problems". *NAFSA Newsletter* 36 (March, 1985): 3, 24.

Teichler, Ulrich and Steube, Wolfgang. "Cost and Financing of Study Abroad Programs". In *Study Abroad in the European Community* (Brussels: European Institute of Education and Social Policy, 1985): 120-145.

The focus of this detailed study is on how the European Community finances study abroad programs. Detailed information concerns the nature of financing, the sources of funds in the various EC countries, and the problems with financing perceived by those involved with the programs.

15. Health

Books

Boer, Evert E. *A Southern Exposure: Cross-Cultural Factors Affecting Health Services Utilization, Psychosomatic Illness and Pre-Departure, Sojourn and Re-Entry Experiences of Foreign Students in North Carolina.* Unpublished Ph.D. Dissertation, University of North Carolina at Chapel Hill, 1983. 256 p. Order No. DA8406876

International students at the University of North Carolina at Chapel Hill and at Duke University were studied before leaving their home countries, in the U.S., and just prior to completing their studies. Problems during the predeparture phase included lack of information and uncertainty about their prospective educational careers. Students interviewed during the sojourn phase reported that their social networks consisted of individuals who were similar in age, student status, and educational goals. They had experienced housing problems, had made few intimate friendships, and felt that their social status in the U.S. was often low. Toward the end of their educational careers they reported they had been given insufficient opportunity to teach or use their foreign or professional skills and had received little encouragement to attend conferences or publish papers. They demonstrated ambivalence toward returning, and they cited continuation of studies, uncertainty of the job market, and indecisiveness as reasons for remaining in the United States.

The findings are discussed using literature from medical anthropology, social psychology, and social epidemiology. Foreign students assemble a social network, of which part--the Transitory Action Set -- is instrumental during their transitory affiliation to U.S. culture. In the discussion of utilization behavior, the influence of social support, somatization, cultural distance, and diagnostic relevance are appraised.

Orientation programs are recommended in all phases of the foreign-student experience; they must respond to the needs of the target population as dictated by age and nationality, and address role and status shock and social relations, among other factors. Health professionals should be made aware of ethnocentric health and counseling services and adapt these to the needs of international students.

Waishwell, Lynn M. *Utilization of Health Services by Four Groups of International Students at Southern Illinois University at Carbondale.* Unpublished Ph.D. Dissertation, Southern Illinois University at Carbondale, 1984. 136 p. Order No. DA8425147

The purpose of this study was to describe the use of local health care services by four groups of international students at Southern Illinois University. The nationalities selected for study were Malaysian, Nigerian, Taiwanese, and Venezuelan. The description provides (1) an indication of the extent to which services are used; (2) an assessment of stated reasons for selection of specific services; (3) sources of information used to select health service; and (4) an examination of the relationships among variables.

The most frequently used health services were items brought from home, the University Health Service, and the local drug store. Rates varied significantly across national groups with respect to use of the Health Service.

Ranking of reasons for selection of health services varied across national groups. The first set of rankings addressed the facility, in which cost was identified as the most important reason. In the second set of rankings, the attitude of the physician was ranked most important.

The most frequently used source of information in selection of health service across national groups was a friend of the same nationality. Other sources varied across national groups.

Articles

Achalu, Onuegbu E. and Duncan, David F. "Drug Taking by Nigerian Students in American Universities: Prevalences for Four Commonly Used Drugs". *International Journal of the Addictions* 19 (May, 1984): 253-263.

Cox, J. L.; Babiker, I. E., and Miller, P. McC. "Psychiatric Problems and First Year Examinations in Overseas Students at Edinburgh University". *Journal of Adolescence* 4 (September, 1981): 261-270.

The relationship between psychiatric illness, lesser degrees of psychiatric symptoms, and first-year examination results in 121 students of foreign nationality or domiciled overseas is described.

Overseas students were reasonably happy at the start of the year. This happiness declined as the winter progressed and picked up again in the Easter term. It was only the happiness level in February that predicted academic failure.

Symptoms of anxiety, depression, and headache during the Easter term were also found to correlate significantly with first-year examination failure. However, only eight students had a definite psychiatric disorder, and only one was referred to the psychiatrist. The practical implications of the findings for organization of student health services are discussed.

Ebbin, Allan J. and Blankenship, Edward S. "A Longitudinal Health Care Study: International Versus Domestic Students". *Journal of American College Health* 34 (February, 1986): 177-182.

The authors reviewed 96,800 diagnoses from student visits to a student health center over a three-year period. Diagnoses coded for international students were compared to those for domestic students. Results are discussed.

Long, Dennis D. "A Cross-Cultural Examination of Fears of Death Among Saudi Arabians". *Omega: Journal of Death and Dying* 16, No. 1 (1985-1986): 43-50.

The article examined factor structure of Hoelter's multidimensional Fear-of-Death Scale, which was translated into Arabic and administered to 84 Saudi Arabian students temporarily living in the United States. The factor structure obtained partially supports the factor structure first obtained for a New Zealand sample.

Van den Broucke, Stephan and Vandereycken, Walter. "Risk Factors for the Development of Eating Disorders in Adolescent Exchange Students: An Exploratory Survey". *Journal of Adolescence* 9 (June, 1986): 145-150.

16. Counseling Services

Books

Carter, R. T. and Sedlacek, W. E. *Needs and Characteristics of Undergraduate International Students* (Research Report No. 1-86). Counseling Center, University of Maryland, 1986. 7 p.

Based on questionnaires completed by 56 entering undergraduate international students, this report examines their needs and characteristics related to their study and life. More than 50% indicated that family members were the most influential persons in their lives. More than 50% indicated an intention to complete their bachelor's degree, and nearly half said that they planned to pursue an advanced degree. The students' educational philosophies were vocational (47%), academic (23%), collegiate (12%), and nonconformist (13%). Most of the students had settled on their vocational goals before coming to college, and the majority indicated that they were quite certain of those goals.

Hashemi, Behnaz. *Attitudes of International Students Toward University Counseling Services.* Ed.D. Dissertation, Texas Southern University, 1985.

Larson, David L. *Counseling Approach Preference of Latin American International Undergraduate Students and U.S. American Undergraduate Students.* Ph.D. Dissertation, University of Kansas, 1984. 91 p. Order No. DA8513801

The main purpose of this study was to find out if Latin American undergraduate students at the University of Kansas significantly preferred one of the two defined counseling approaches. In Approach A the counselor acted in a non-directive manner, stressed client verbalization, and placed heavy responsibility on the client for solving the client's problem. In Approach B the counselor acted in a directive manner, supplied pragmatic information/help, and emphasized shared counselor-client responsibility in solving the client's problem. A secondary purpose for this study was to discern if Latin American international students differed significantly in counseling approach preference from a comparison sample of U.S. American undergraduate students at the University of Kansas.

Leong, Fredrick T. L. *Counseling International Students -- Relevant Resources in High Interest Areas.* Ann Arbor, MI: University of Michigan, School of Education, ERIC Clearinghouse on Counseling and Personnel Services, 1984.

Lomak, Paul P. *An Investigation of Foreign Students' Awareness, Utilization and Satisfaction with Selected Student Personnel Services and Programs at Ohio University, Athens 1983/84.* Unpublished Ph.D. Dissertation, Ohio University, 1984. 195 p. Order No. DA8504158

The study examines the extent of foreign students' awareness, usage, and satisfaction with selected student personnel services and programs based on dependent variables of age, sex, quarters of enrollment, marital status, university rank, and regional origin.

Generally, a low level of awareness, usage, and satisfaction with most services and programs of student personnel was determined through the data analysis. About half of the students are unaware of leadership and cultural workshops; counseling on career alternatives; counseling on health problems; workshops on nutrition and drug abuse; cross-cultural and personal adjustment; counseling on study habits and examination fears; practical training; and traveling instructions.

Services used by more than half of the students included registration; immigration and visa matters; health; orientation; and aspects of Housing and Food. More than 40 percent of the students are satisfied with all services stated above with the exception of Housing and Food. Statistical differences for the 31 selected services or programs varied from 1 to 12. Thus, all the null hypotheses are accepted, meaning that the dependent variables previously stated are not factors in levels of awareness, usage, and satisfaction by foreign students.

Manese, Jeanne E., et al. *Needs and Perceptions of Female and Male International Undergraduate Students.* College Park, MD: University of Maryland, College Park Counselling Center, 1984. 14 p.

Pedersen, P., ed. *Handbook of Cross-Cultural Counseling and Therapy.* Westport, CT: Greenwood Press, 1985.

Pyle, Richard K., ed. *Guiding the Development of Foreign Students.* San Francisco, CA: Jossey-Bass, 1986.

This collection of essays focuses on student services aspects. Among the essays are "The Foreign Student and Student Life", by Richard Feiff and Margaret Kidd, "Advising and Counseling the International Student", by Ron Cadieux and Bea Wehrly, and

"The Future of International Student Development", by Barbara Clark and Richard Pyle. The essays are fairly general in nature, but will be of interest to those involved in student advisement and related fields. Separate summaries are provided for each of the essays elsewhere in this bibliography.

Samuda, Ronald J. and Wolfgang, Aaron, eds. *Intercultural Counseling and Assessment: Global Perspective*. Lewiston, NY: C. J. Hogrefe, 1985. 408 p.

While this book does not deal directly with foreign students, it will be relevant to those involved with counseling people in a cross-cultural environment, including foreign students. This volume is a collection of essays focusing on cross-cultural counseling. Among its concerns is the relationship between immigration patterns and counseling/adjustment issues (using Canada, the United States, and Australia as key countries for immigration). Perspectives on intercultural counseling from the U.S., Britain, and Germany are considered. Additional chapters deal with the testing of minority groups, cognitive strategies, and the counseling of learning-impaired minority students.

Articles

Anderson, Thomas R. and Myer, Thomas E. "Presenting Problems, Counselor Contacts, and 'No Shows': International and American College Students". *Journal of College Student Personnel* 26 (November, 1985): 500-503.

A review of case files spanning one academic year at a university-affiliated counseling center showed that 40 international students had sought counseling services during the year. Forty case files on American students were chosen at random to compare with the international student files. Problems were diagnosed according to the third edition of the Diagnostic and Statistical Manual of Mental Disorders. Chi-square and tests revealed no differences between the two groups in the nature of problems, number of contacts, or length of time of counseling. However, international students had a higher rate of dropping out after initial contact than did the American students.

Cadieux, Ron A. L. and Wehrly, Bea. "Advising and Counseling the International Student". In *Guiding the Development of Foreign Students*, ed. K. Pyle (San Francisco, London: Jossey-Bass, 1986): 51-64.

The chapter reviews special areas to be considered in assisting foreign students with curricular planning and personal and emotional problems. It identifies five most common concerns of international students from developing countries: language difficulties; financial problems; adjustment to a new educational system; social and cultural adjustment; and relevance of academic programs. It stresses that advising and counseling international students requires awareness of the adaptation period experienced by sojourners in a foreign country, sensitivity to the powerful impact of culture on behavior, and willingness to empathize with the value system of international students.

Clark, Barbara A. and Pyle, K. Richard. "The Future of International Student Development". In *Guiding the Development of Foreign Students*, ed. K. Pyle (San Francisco, London: Jossey-Bass, 1986): 83-87.

Das, Ajit K., et al. "The Counseling Needs of Foreign Students". *International Journal for Advancement of Counseling* 9, No. 2 (1986): 167-174.

The article reports the results of three studies of the counseling needs of international students at the University of Minnesota, Duluth. It provides a historical perspective on the changes in students' needs and puts forward some program recommendations that may enhance the quality of foreign student experience while adding a valuable dimension to the educational experience of American students.

Day, R. C. and Hajj, F. M. "Delivering Counseling Services to International Students: The Experience of the American University of Beirut". *Journal of College Student Personnel* 27, No. 4 (1986): 353-357.

Eto, K. "Foreign Graduate Students in Japan; The Counselor's View". *Japan Quarterly* 32 (January/March, 1985): 58-60.

Idowu, Adeyemi I. "Counseling Nigerian Students in United States Colleges and Universities". *Journal of Counseling and Development* 63, No. 8 (April, 1985): 506-509.

> The author discusses ways in which American counselors can build positive relationships and initiate appropriate interventions with Nigerian students on their college and university campuses.

Locke, Don C. and Velasco, Jacqueline. "Hospitality Begins with the Invitation: Counselling Foreign Students". *Journal of Multicultural Counseling and Development* 15 (July, 1987): 115-119.

Wehrly, B. "Counseling International Students: Issues, Concerns and Programs". *International Journal for the Advancement of Counseling* 9, No. 1 (1986): 11-22.

17. Adaptation Problems

Books

Amoh, Kwabena O. *Newly Arrived Foreign Students at a U.S. University: Their Adjustment Difficulties and Coping Strategies.* Unpublished Ph.D. Dissertation, University of Minnesota, 1984. 191 p. Order No. DA8424662

> A longitudinal study was conducted on 64 newly arrived foreign students at the University of Minnesota. This randomly selected respondent group was studied throughout academic year 1982-83.

The findings of the study showed that academically their most common problems are: (a) lack of effective communication skill in English; (b) frequency of college/university examinations at the University of Minnesota; (c) concerns about grades; (d) lack of knowledge about student/faculty relationships in the U.S.; and (e) comprehending registration procedures at the University of Minnesota.

Social problems could be summarized as follows: (a) concern about understanding American "slang" words; (b) concern about being understood by Americans; (c) loneliness, and negative remarks and attitudes from some American students.

Personal problems were (a) financial difficulties; (b) tension of adjustment to different environment; (c) locating suitable housing at reasonable prices; and (d) time-budgeting in the U.S.

Most of the coping strategies of the students remained the same throughout the academic year, and coping strategies were necessary tools to either solving or improving adjustment difficulties in a new environment.

Bradley, D. and Bradley, M. *Problems of Asian Students in Australia: Language, Culture and Education.* Canberra: Australian Government Publishing Service, 1984.

This useful study focuses on the language problems of students from Thailand, Malaysia, and Indonesia studying in Australia. Most of the book is concerned with a discussion of these linguistic problems, but several chapters also deal with cultural and social problems of foreign students in Australia. The research is based on in-depth interviews with fifty students. A number of recommendations are made on the basis of the study:

1. There needs to be more preparation in English by foreign students coming to Australia, with a stress on spoken and written English rather than rules of grammar.
2. Graded self-instructional materials should be available.

3. There should be handbooks on study in Australia available overseas.
4. Study skills orientations should be available.

Bristow, Rupert and Shotnes, Stephen, eds. *Overseas Students -- At Home in Britain?* London: United Kingdom Council on Overseas Student Affairs, 1987.

How do overseas students feel about the time they spend in Britain? What kind of welcome is provided for them? How does British society treat them? This volume presents five of the winning entries from the Friends of UKCOSA essay competition for overseas students. The authors come from a wide variety of backgrounds, and so present a broad cross-section of student opinion about their experiences in the U.K., both good and bad. In addition to the student essays, three scholars (Kazim Bacchus, Anthony Parsons and Alastair Niven) add their own broader perspectives. The student essays are generally personal reactions to life in Britain and British universities.

Hamouda, Rabi Ahmed I. *A Case Study of Academic and Socio-Cultural Adjustment Problems of Graduate International Students: Recommendations for Curriculum Development.* Ph.D. Dissertation, University of Pittsburgh, 1986. 199 p. Order No. DA8701964

The purpose of this interpretive case study was to identify the academic and socio-cultural adjustment problems of a specific group of international students and make curricular recommendations to aid international students in their adjustment.

The case study revealed seven categories of problems with academic adjustment: (1) adviser-related difficulties; (2) curriculum/program relevance; (3) discrimination; (4) educational system differences; (5) instructor-related difficulties; (6) language proficiency; and (7) university-system difficulties.

Eight categories of socio-cultural adjustment problems were found: (1) American-system differences; (2) American values and customs; (3) discrimination; (4) ethnocentrism; (5) finances; (6) housing; (7) language proficiency; and (8) social isolation.

A general description of the international student was provided. The Tylerian rationale for curriculum development served as the framework for the development of curricular recommendations. The curricular recommendations addressed the identified academic and socio-cultural needs of students.

Hsu, Lorie Ro Ping. *Loneliness in Foreign Students and Depressed Clients*. Unpublished Ph.D. Dissertation, University of Southern Mississippi, 1983. 131 p. Order No. DA8414922

Loneliness has been demonstrated to be related to and distinguished from depression. This research attempted to further clarify the relationships between loneliness and depression in a clinically depressed client group and a socially alienated foreign-student group. Two comparison groups (American college students and college students in Taiwan) were used. Weiss' (1973) theory postulating two forms of loneliness -- emotionally isolated loneliness and socially isolated loneliness -- was adopted; and the UCLA Loneliness Scale (1978), the Belcher Extended Loneliness Scale (1973), and the Beck Depression Inventory (1972) were used as measurements. One hundred and thirty-one foreign Chinese students, 21 outpatient depressed clients, 44 American college students, and 41 Chinese college students served as four groups of subjects. Results showed that although loneliness is related to depression, loneliness is a different syndrome from depression. Depressed clients scored significantly higher than all other groups on measures of both types of loneliness as well as depression. Foreign students felt significantly more socially isolated loneliness compared to both American students and students in their native country, but these socially isolated lonely students did not feel significant amounts of either emotionally isolated loneliness or depression. Within foreign students, married students felt less loneliness than single students. Various kinds of loneliness-coping strategies were discussed. Questions about cross-cultural differences of loneliness experiences and loneliness-coping strategies were also discussed.

Laila, Yousef Abu. *Integration und Entfremdung. Zur Situation Auslandischer Studenten in der Bundesrepublik Deutschland (Integration and Alienation: The Situation of Foreign Students in the Federal Republic of Germany).* Göttingen: Edition Heridot, 1981. 218 p.

This dissertation is based on thirty interviews and the evaluation of sixty questionnaires, as well as five group discussions with African and Asian students at the universities in Clausthal-Zellerfeld and Göttingen from 1976 to 1978. The topics and issues discussed include the students' reasons for studying abroad; their first impressions and experiences in the Federal Republic; and their studies, social contacts, and relationship to their own countries. Language difficulties, housing problems, and academic advisement emerged as the most important problems.

Liu, Zaida Vega. *A Cross-Cultural Study of Depression Among Foreign Graduate Students from Six Selected Areas.* Ed.D. Dissertation, George Peabody College for Teachers of Vanderbilt University, 1985. 168 p. Order No. DA8517423

This study explored the difference in depression and symptomatology of depression of six groups of graduate international students (Arab, Chinese from Taiwan, Indian, Japanese, Korean from South Korea, and Latin American) enrolled at Vanderbilt University during the fall of 1984. The study also explored the relationship between depression and sex, age, marital status, and length of stay in the U.S. in the total sample of 137 and within each individual subsample. Students were administered a personal data sheet and the Zung Self-Rating Depression Scale (Zung, 1965).

No significant difference was found between the means for the six groups on the depression measure and on depressive symptomatology. No significant relationship was found between

depression and sex, age, marital status, and length of stay in the
U.S. However, at the level of each individual subgroup, some
significance was detected. The Japanese subsample showed high
correlation between depression and marital status. The same
held true for depression and length of stay in the U.S. in the
Chinese subsample. A high negative correlation was found
between depression and age in the Japanese subsample. Of the
sample, 32.5% scored above 50 in the measure of depression (SDS
Index), indicating the presence of mild to moderate and marked
to severe depression.

Meloni, Christine F. *Adjustment Problems of Foreign Students in U.S.
Colleges and Universities.* Washington, D.C.: ERIC Clearinghouse
on Languages and Linguistics, 1986. 4 p.

United States colleges and universities can play a major role in
facilitating foreign students' adjustment to life in a new culture.
The foreign students' most common problems include
homesickness, finances, housing and food, English language
proficiency, understanding lectures and participating in class
discussion, preparing written and oral reports, understanding
American social customs, and making friends and acceptance in
social groups. The major variables affecting their adjustment are
national origin, undergraduate versus graduate status, sex,
marital status, and major field of study. Institutions can ease the
adjustment process by making available English language
instruction, orientation programs, counseling, and host-family
programs.

Mickle, Kathryn M. *The Cross-Cultural Adaptation of Hong Kong
Students at Two Ontario Universities.* Unpublished Ph.D.
Dissertation, University of Toronto, 1984.

Students from Hong Kong have experienced problems in adapting
to North American university life. This study was designed to
investigate the influence of certain factors on the cross-cultural
adaptation of these students. The hypotheses predicted that
successful adaptation is related to the number of Canadian
friends, the amount of participation in activities with

Canadians, tolerance of ambiguity, length of stay, perceived lack of discrimination, and less-strong identification with traditional Chinese culture.

Questionnaires were sent to a random sample of undergraduates studying on student visas at the University of Toronto and York University. One hundred and eighty-seven questionnaires were analyzed, including 48 from students attending ESL classes at both universities, selected as a sample of convenience. Fifteen students were interviewed for a better understanding of the results.

Adaptation was measured by the students' self-reported satisfaction with their ability to speak English and with their sojourn, and by the number of problems and stresses.

The findings support the hypotheses that adaptation is positively correlated to number of Canadian friends, participation in activities with Canadians, and a longer stay in Canada. Less traditional students also adapt more successfully, as do those who have not experienced discrimination.

Results from the tolerance of ambiguity scale were discarded for statistical reasons, but in the questionnaires and interviews, students mentioned openness and flexibility (related to tolerance of ambiguity) as important qualities.

A multiple regression analysis found that the most important variables to explain adaptation are traditionality, lack of discrimination, year of study, ease in making friends with Canadians, and finding Canadians kind.

Findings of this study confirm the "modified cultural contact hypothesis", which argues that foreign students satisfied and comfortable with their interactions with local people and the local culture will indicate more general satisfaction with their sojourn. The findings also confirm that length of stay and lack of discrimination are important indicators of adaptation, and that students who are less traditional adapt more successfully.

The present study adds to the literature on the adaptation of foreign students and Chinese students in particular. The study concludes with practical suggestions for aiding the adaptation of these students.

Mickle, Kathryn and Chan, Rosanna. *The Cross-Cultural Adaptation of Hong Kong Chinese Students at Canadian Universities*. Ottawa: Canadian Bureau for International Education, 1986.

The study is designed to investigate the influence of certain psychological and sociological factors on the adaptation of Chinese undergraduates from Hong Kong at universities across Canada. It confirms that successful adaptation of visa students from Hong Kong is linked to such factors like participation in activities with Canadians, a longer stay in the country, lack of perceived discrimination, and some aspects of non-traditionality. In order for universities to better facilitate foreign students in the adaptation process, the study makes the following recommendations:

1. programs or handbooks should be provided to give accurate information about foreign students, their cultures, and their possible difficulties in studying in Canada so as to increase the awareness level of the academic community at large;

2. foreign students should also be given handbooks and orientation covering Canadian life, customs, applicable policies and regulations, the types of problems foreign students commonly face, and general information regarding day-to-day living;

3. assistance should be provided to help find lodging for these students;

4. intensive and relevant courses in English should be offered to lessen the language barrier;

5. support groups and peer counseling should be established to help foreign students overcome difficulties;

6. all personnel dealing with students must have some training in intercultural sensitivity.

Omar, Ali Abbullah. *Problems of International Students As Perceived by International Students and Faculty in a Public University.* Ph.D. Dissertation, North Texas State University, 1985.

Paez, Georgia S. *The Student Service Related to Problems of International and English As a Second Language Students in a Selected Community College.* Unpublished Ph.D. Dissertation, North Texas State University, 1985. 266 p. Order No. DA8604571

The study focused on the student-service-related problems of culturally distinct groups of students attending a community college. The groups selected for the study were sixty international students and sixty English As a Second Language (ESL) students. The researcher administered the Michigan International Student Problem Inventory, an instrument that has been widely used to indicate foreign students' problems. Combining the use of naturalistic research methodology, the researcher utilized an in-depth interview to document the problems they were facing. Patterns and trends among the problems were analyzed and reported. The results indicated that many international students experienced concerns in the area of financial aid, had difficulties with immigration regulations and work restrictions, and experienced forms of racial and social discrimination. The ESL students tended to experience most difficulties in the area of English-language functioning, but also experienced problems related to academic functioning and making friends. The student service areas most closely related to the international students' concerns were Financial Aid, Admissions, Placement, Counseling, and English Language Services. ESL students' problems were most closely related to the areas of English Language Services, Admissions, Counseling, and Academic Advisement. Recommendations generated by the study include the development of a new instrument to include topics identified by the students in the open-ended section of the questionnaire, a translation of the instrument into the major languages of the ESL population, and the need for future research on subgroups of the populations who indicated a greater number of problems than the others. Institutional recommendations are included which focus on how the college could address the problems that the students identified.

Ramos De Perez, J. Maria. *An Exploratory Study of Adjustment Difficulties of Spanish-Speaking International Students to Study at an American University.* Ed.D. Dissertation, University of Cincinnati, 1985. 194 p. Order No. DA8518145

Fifty-one Spanish-speaking international students were surveyed to identify adjustment problems they faced at the University of Cincinnati. Eight of the surveyed students were also interviewed to illuminate survey results with anecdotes and personal experiences.

The greatest adjustment problems resulted from lack of familiarity with the English language and lack of social contact with Americans. Some differences in adjustment problems were attributable to age, length of time in the United States, degree level being sought, sex, whether it was a first sojourn away from home, and length of previous sojourns.

Recommendations were made concerning ways to improve the language training and social integration of international students.

Ramos-Ruiz, Zobeida. *The Adaptation of Spanish-Speaking Latin American Graduate Students to the United States Higher Education Professor.* Ph.D. Dissertation, Michigan State University, 1985. 163 p. Order No. DA8513935

This study attempted to gather information on (1) the students' perception of the role of the Latin American higher-education professor; (2) perceptions of the role of the United States higher-education professor; (3) expectations of the United States higher-education professor; (4) description of their adaptation process to the United States higher-education professor; and (5) the students' actions and recommendations on how to adapt to the United States higher-education professor.

Latin American professors were described as more oriented toward individual students. United States professors were described as tending to utilize an analytic/synthetic approach in their instruction, more organized and clear in their explanations, and more dynamic and enthusiastic in their teaching. Latin American and United States higher education professors had one characteristic in common: their respect of students as persons.

Data illustrated that students expected, prior to arriving in the United States, the United States higher-education professor to prefer group to individual teaching, to know worldwide education, to require absolute discipline, to be challenged by the students' superiority, and to be always accessible. However, among these characteristics, students identified that knowing worldwide education was not descriptive of the United States higher-education professor.

The students' adaptation process to the United States higher-education professor was described as interesting, stimulating, and satisfactory, as well as somewhat frustrating and difficult. Students took two types of actions to adapt to the United States higher-education professor. They attempted either to relate to professors or to isolate themselves. Students strongly recommended that others be open and communicate with professors and other students to facilitate adaptation.

Recommendations are offered to sponsoring institutions to enhance the students' ability to cope with the educational environment of the United States higher education institutions, and to United States higher education institutions and professors to train personnel to effectively relate with foreign students and institute programs and courses having an international perspective. Further research is called for that includes conducting similar studies to examine different populations of students and to examine the cross-cultural validity of the instrumentation.

Shore, William Benn. *Differences in Adjustment of Vietnamese, Indian and Latin American International Students at a Mid-Atlantic Community College.* Ph.D. Dissertation, University of Georgia, 1986.

Vaz, Pelgy. *Stress, Adjustment and Social Relations of Foreign Students.* Unpublished Ph.D. Dissertation, University of Nebraska, 1984. 172 p. Order No. DA8423838

This study examines some social and psychological effects of international study in a population of foreign students studying at the University of Nebraska, Lincoln. Data collected from 285 foreign students attending the same university were analyzed to examine cross-cultural differences and their impacts on stress, adjustment, and social relations.

Contact with citizens of the host country is an important variable: the greater the contact the foreign student has with the host country, the lower the level of his/her stress and anxiety. Those students who perceive themselves to have greater cultural similarity with the host country are likely to enjoy more social contacts within the host country.

Articles

Adelegan, Francis O. and Parks, David J. "Problem of Transition for African Students in an American University". *Journal of College Student Personnel* 26 (November, 1985): 504-508.

The authors surveyed black East African, black West African and Arabic North African students enrolled in an American university to identify their problems and personal attributes and environmental conditions influencing their experience. The article discusses social, transportation, food, loneliness, and other problems.

Bendersky, Nora, et al. "Coping with Transitions". *Journal of College Student Personnel* 25 (November, 1984): 555-556.

The article describes a workshop for nine South American students at the Hebrew University of Jerusalem. The two-day session focussed on exploring coping behavior that could help students adjust to transitions.

Chinapah, V. "Higher Education in Sweden: Policies and Institutional Arrangements: A Brief Account of Social Integration Processes and the Social Life of Foreign Students from Third World Countries". *Higher Education in Europe* 11, No. 3 (1986): 24-30.

This article deals with the integration and the social life of foreign students, specifically from Africa, in the course of their undergraduate studies in Sweden. The conclusions drawn from African students, and the evidence derived from a number of evaluation studies conducted in Sweden, indicate that other groups of students such as immigrants, political refugees, and non-Africans are confronted with similar problems. These problems include: educational legislation, learning environment, counseling, information, and social services. The article also examines the existing policies and provides suggestions to alleviate the problems encountered by foreign students.

Chittiwatanapong, Prasert. "An Evaluation of Study in Japan". *Research in Higher Education (Daigaku Ronshu)* No. 15 (1986): 33-46.

A former recipient of a Japanese government scholarship and now a university lecturer teaching Japanese subjects, the author evaluates his experience in Japan as positive and valuable. However, he also points out the difficulties in studying in Japan, namely the Japanese language and the unfamiliar teaching style of the Japanese professors.

Dyal, J. A. and Chan, C. "Stress and Distress: A Study of Hong Kong Chinese and Euro-Canadian Students". *Journal of Cross-Cultural Psychology* No. 16 (December, 1985).

The Marlowe-Crowne Social Desirability Scale, the Problems of Living Adjustment Scale, and nine items of the Spielberger's exam-anxiety scale were completed by 100 Chinese students at the University of Hong Kong, 39 Hong Kong Chinese students at the University of Waterloo, Canada, and 112 Euro-Canadian students at the University of Waterloo. Analysis of covariance, controlling for social desirability scores, and t-tests revealed that the Chinese women in both groups reported more symptoms on the distress scale than did the Euro-Canadian women and more symptoms than did the Chinese men. Few differences were found among the groups on stressful life events and test anxiety. Bivariate correlations indicated differing patterns of relationships among the variables depending on the gender and cultural group.

Eng, Law Lee and Manthei, Robert J. "Malaysian and New Zealand Students' Self-Reported Adjustment and Academic Performance". *New Zealand Journal of Educational Studies* 19 (November, 1984): 179-184.

This study is intended to gauge the extent to which the largest group of overseas students at the University of Canterbury, Malaysians, considered the following factors to have influenced their academic performance: (1) accommodation; (2) language; (3) finance; (4) educational experience; and (5) social adjustment. Also, the study examines whether the problems experienced by the Malaysian students are typical of foreign students at Canterbury. A total of 160 questionnaires were distributed to Malaysian students and 100 to New Zealand students. The results of the survey indicate that while overseas students may have some adjustment difficulties at university, New Zealand students share similar difficulties. The results challenge widely-held assumptions about the needs of overseas students.

Goudy, Frank W. and Moushey, Eugene. "Library Instruction and Foreign Students: A Survey of Opinions and Practices Among Selected Libraries". *Reference Librarian* 10 (Spring-Summer, 1984): 15-26.

Heikinheimo, P. S. and Shute, J. C. M. "The Adaptation of Foreign Students: Student Views and Institutional Implications". *Journal of College Student Personnel* 27 (September, 1986): 399-406.

At a Canadian university with more than 1,000 foreign students, data on foreign student adaptation were gathered through structured/unstructured interviews and participation observation for 46 African and Southeast-Asian students. The students identified problems in areas of language, academic matters, culture, racial discrimination, and social interaction. Both groups felt heavy pressure to perform well academically, usually due to family expectations. Consequently, most of them believed that they studied more extensively than did Canadian students. Forty-two of the 46 foreign students reported encounters with subtle forms of racial discrimination. Social interaction patterns varied according to individuals and groups. On the whole, they were either somewhat integrated or somewhat isolated.

Hossain, Najmul and La Berge, Bernard. "Psychological Costs of U.S. Education for Foreign Students: An Empirical Test". *Journal of International Student Personnel* 2, No. 2 (1985): 21-23.

Hsu, L. R., et al. "Cultural and Emotional Components of Loneliness and Depression". *Journal of Psychology* 121 (January, 1987): 61-70.

Kwack, Young Woo. "Evaluating Study in Japan". *Research in Higher Education (Daigaku Ronshu)* No. 15 (1986): 79-83.

Oyen, Orjar. "The Integration of Foreign Students". *CRE-Information* 57 (1982): 45-59.

Reiff, Richard F. and Kidd, Margaret A. "The Foreign Student and Student Life". In *Guiding the Development of Foreign Students*, ed. K. Pyle (San Francisco: Jossey-Bass, 1986): 39-50.

The authors review methods that lead to the effective assimilation of foreign students into campus life and describe proved techniques and systems of assisting the foreign students to become a part of the total institution: orientation, intercultural exchange, educational enrichment, and intercultural communication. They also point out that the institution is obligated to fulfill certain needs and to consider the special needs when it accepts a foreign student and when it plans programs and activities since these can have a significant impact on the quality of foreign students.

Robinson, N. M. and Janos, P. M. "Psychological Adjustment in a College-Level Program of Marked Academic Acceleration". *Journal of Youth and Adolescence* No. 15 (February, 1986): 51-60.

Surdam, Joyce C. and Collins, James R. "Adaptation of International Students: A Cause for Concern". *Journal of College Student Personnel* 25 (May, 1984): 240-245.

Investigated the adaptation of 143 international students in relation to individual and family variables. Results suggested successful adaptation was related to spending leisure time with Americans, adequate knowledge of English, better educated families, and religious participation. Use of student services was infrequent.

Sykes, Israel J. and Eden, Dov. "Transitional Stress, Social Support and Psychological Strain". *Journal of Occupational Behavior* 6 (October, 1985): 293-298.

Vogel, Suzanne H. "Toward Understanding the Adjustment Problems of Foreign Families in the College Community: The Case of Japanese Wives at the Harvard University Health Services". *Journal of American College Health* 34 (June, 1986): 274-279.

Asians alone comprise one-third of all foreign students at Harvard University, and 10% of all foreign scholars come from Japan. This article deals with Japanese wives at Harvard University Health Services in attempt to increase awareness of the nature of the problems facing foreign families in the college community. Data are collected from two discussion groups of international wives: one composed entirely of Japanese women speaking Japanese, and the other including women from all countries, speaking English as the common language. The problem of language, a primary problem for Japanese women to get along in the U.S., is discussed in relation to the social contexts or the interpersonal relationships in the two countries. The pervasive anxiety of living overseas is analyzed in view of the cultural identity of the Japanese. Loneliness, resulting from social isolation, is the biggest problem of many Japanese women. The circumstances of daily living have an impact on family relationships. The relationship between university health services and Japanese families is discussed. The author concludes that many adjustment problems are inevitable and normal, and that Americans should keep their minds open to things and ideas of other cultures.

Wong-Rieger, Durhane. "Testing a Model of Emotional and Coping Responses to Problems in Adaptation: Foreign Students at a Canadian University". *International Journal of Intercultural Relations* 8, No. 2 (1984): 153-184.

Develops and tests a model of cross-cultural adaptation that proposes that adaptation to movement across cultures involves three processes: learning new social norms, matching behavior to these norms, and matching one's self-concept to the newly acquired behaviors and social norms. Examines the hypothesized relationship between mismatch problems, affective response, and coping strategy. Finds that subjects' interpretations agreed with the mismatches proposed by the model and that their reported affective and coping responses confirmed the majority of the hypothesized relationships. Concludes that the mismatch model may serve as a good framework for classifying diverse adaptation problems and for predicting the coping strategies that would effectively resolve these problems.

18. Academic Performance

Books

Aseeri, Ali Saeed. *The Prediction of Foreign Graduate Students' Academic Achievement at Michigan State University.* Ph.D. Dissertation, Michigan State University, 1985. 273 p. Order No. DA8520497

The main purpose of this study was to determine the extent to which the foreign student index of previous academic achievement (IPAA), average of their English scores on the MSU English Test (MSU-AETS), GPA 1-term, and demographic information can predict their graduate academic success in MSU graduate schools, as measured by GPAs, academic credit load, and adviser's rating of the doctoral student's academic competence. To maintain adequate control over the sources of heterogeneity of the foreign student population, the study sample included all foreign graduate students enrolled in MSU graduate schools between fall term 1978 and spring term 1982 who had completed at least 12 credits.

Although the predictors differed with respect to the magnitude of their validity coefficient for the various groups, the overall findings suggested that the prediction of foreign graduate students' academic success is possible from the available preadmission data. Based on the findings of the various analyses, the following conclusions were drawn: (1) MSU-AETS was a good predictor of foreign students' academic success, particularly of those students from non-English-speaking countries; (2) IPAA appeared to exhibit an encouraging sign as a predictor of foreign students' academic success as measured by GPA; (3) GPA 1-term was the best single predictor that yielded a consistent validity coefficient with all the defined criterion measures; (4) GPA 1-term, MSU-AETS, and college type were the best predictors of foreign students' academic achievement, as measured by GPA; (5) accurate prediction of foreign graduate students' academic success should result from separate validation on a homogeneous group rather than validation on a heterogeneous group.

Beane, Bonnie A. *A Model for Foreign Student Retention and Attrition: A Case Study of SUNY-Buffalo.* Unpublished Ph.D. Dissertation, State University of New York at Buffalo, 1985. 161 p. Order No. DA8510311

This dissertation examines the relationship(s) among a variety of pre-admission selection criteria utilized by the Office of Foreign Admissions at the State University of New York at Buffalo for selecting undergraduate foreign students. The independent variables examined were English proficiency, secondary educational background, prior postsecondary educational experience, QPA, gender, and major field of study. The students' financial status was also reviewed, but it was not included in the statistical analysis. The dependent variable was retention/attrition.

The goal of this study was to discover the combination of factors that would best predict academic achievement and, therefore, retention. A model of retention was developed from the analysis.

Students who were transfers either from abroad or from within the United States were more likely to be retained than freshman students. Engineering and business majors were more likely to be retained than other majors. If the student's secondary and/or postsecondary educational background were compatible with the college major, he or she was more likely to be retained than if they were disparate. Undecided majors had high attrition rates.

English proficiency is essential to academic success. However, its importance varies in terms of the requirements of the particular major.

Eghbali, Iraj. *Stress and Academic Performance of International Students.* Ph.D. Dissertation, University of Missouri-Columbia, 1985. 113 p. Order No. DA8611734

Purpose. The purpose of this study was to investigate the relationship between academic performance of international students as demonstrated by students' GPA and the selected variables of stress (as indicated by life change events), age, nationality grouping, gender, and length of stay in the United States. The relationship between stress and the other predictor variables was also investigated.

Findings and Conclusions. (1) For undergraduate international students at the University of Missouri-Columbia greater life change, assumed to be a cause of stress, was associated with lower GPAs. The relationship has been described as "small effect size." (2) The best combination of predictors of GPA for undergraduate international students consists of that measure of stress, length of stay in the United States, age, and gender. A profile of higher achievers might consist of older females whose length of stay in the United States is less than five years and who have not experienced the "high" stress-producing events in their lives. (3) The negative correlation that is referred to "small effect size" between stress and nationality (African) and age suggests that younger, male African undergraduates experience fewer stress-producing life changes than the other subgroups sampled. (4) The significant positive relationship between Iranian graduate students and stress suggests that Iranian graduate students experience more stress-producing life changes than other nationality groups. (5) Older undergraduate international students achieve higher academically than their younger counterparts even though they experience more life-change stress. (6) Female undergraduate international students appear to experience greater stress-producing life changes than males, however they are higher achievers academically.

Isoplan-Gross, Bernd and Zwick, Martin. *Studienabbruch bei Studenten aus Entwicklungslandern in der BRD. Umfang, Ursachen,*

Folgen (Dropouts Among Students From the Developing Countries Studying in the FRG). Saarbrucken: CIM, 1982. 212 p.

This statistical analysis, conducted from 1979 to 1981, revealed that the dropout rate among students from developing countries is about 22%. This contradicts earlier studies that held that the dropout rate was 51%. The 22% dropout rate translates into 700 to 800 students per year who need special help, especially those in mathematics and the natural sciences but also economics and the social sciences. Reasons for dropping out include insecurity, family problems, and fear of failure. Most of the dropouts do not want to return to their home countries.

Mustafa, Ali Hajjan. *A Study of Academic Problems Encountered by Saudi Students at Western Michigan University.* Ed.D. Dissertation, Western Michigan University, 1985.

Pharis, Keith E. *A Study of Faculty Perceptions of Foreign Graduate Student Writing.* Ph.D. Dissertation, University of Illinois at Urbana-Champaign, 1987.

Shotnes, Stephen, ed. *The Teaching and Tutoring of Overseas Students. Report of a Workshop.* London: United Kingdom Council on Overseas Students Affairs, 1985.

Wilson, Kenneth M. *Factors Affecting GMAT Predictive Validity for Foreign MBA Students: An Exploratory Study. Research Report.* Princeton, NJ: Educational Testing Service, 1985. 96 p.

Wilson, Kenneth M. *Foreign Nationals Taking the GRE General Testing during 1981-82 -- Selected Characteristics and Test Performance.* Princeton, NJ: Educational Testing Service, 1984.

Articles

Ball, Mary Alice and Mahony, Molly. "Foreign Students, Libraries, and Culture". *College and Research Libraries* 48 (March, 1987): 160-166.

The article discusses the special needs of foreign students in academic libraries, with a special focus on bibliographic instruction and research skills. To meet these needs, strategies are suggested for identifying students who need special instruction; teaching research methods; increasing staff sensitivity; and designing a staff development workshop.

Barnes, Leslie R. "The Negotiation of Grades As a Central Feature of an Educational Exchange Program". *College and University* 59 (Winter, 1984): 136-149.

This article investigates the grading of students in an American university -- Yankee State University -- and the grading of the same students when they continue their studies abroad in a British college -- Hadini College. The article looks at existing critiques of the grading system in the U.S. and focuses on the problems that exchange programs pose for faculty and students in coping with different cultural and institutional norms and rules, specifically with regard to grading.

Dunnett, Stephen C. "Current Communicative Needs of Foreign Students in the College/University Classroom". *International Programs Quarterly (SUNY)* 1 (Winter, 1985): 22-26.

Spinks, J. A. and Ho, D. Y. F. "Chinese Students at an English-Language University: Prediction of Academic Performance". *Higher Education* 13 (December, 1984): 657-674.

This study reviews evidence collected over the past two to fifteen years that relates to the issue of prediction of academic performance of Chinese students at an English-language and Western-oriented university -- the University of Hong Kong. This review is complemented by an analysis of data collected longitudinally over a five year period, using multiple regression analyses, path analysis, and canonical correlation analyses. The results provide evidence of factors that are important in determining the ability of a student to adapt to the foreign cultural and language barriers that exist at this university. In particular, ability in English language and mathematics provides good and reasonably independent predictors of success. The data show the importance of considering cultural background of students when assessing their aptitude for study, and offer information for Western universities regarding their admission procedures for Chinese students.

Wayman, Sally G. "The International Students in the Academic Library". *Journal of Academic Leadership* 9 (January, 1984): 336-341.

The discussion of problems of the international student in American higher education highlights communication (cultural differences, nonverbals), learning styles and behaviors (questioning vs. imitation, group vs. individual success, classroom conduct), and knowledge of libraries (self-sufficiency). Recommendations for improving the librarian/foreign student encounter are also discussed.

19. The Foreign Teaching Assistant

Books

Bailey, Kathleen; Pialorsi, Frank, and Zukowski, Jean, eds. *Foreign Teaching Assistants in U.S. Universities*. Washington, D.C.: National Association for Foreign Student Affairs, 1984. 133 p.

The first full-scale consideration of the role of the foreign student as a teaching assistant in American higher education, this edited volume provides several different perspectives on the topic. Chapters relate to such problems as language competence and communication skills of foreign teaching assistants and the classroom culture and foreign teaching assistants. Several chapters discuss programs to assist foreign teaching assistants. These chapters include an overview of the programs aimed at foreign teaching assistants in the U.S., and descriptions of a one-day workshop, a week-long language skills program, and a semester-long workshop. Several concluding chapters discuss the evaluation of programs and appropriate instruments for measuring linguistic and communication skills.

Davis, Brian Kenneth. *A Study of the Effectiveness of Training for Foreign Teaching Assistants.* Ph.D. Dissertation, The Ohio State University, 1984. 270 p. Order No. DA8418931

The quasi-experimental study investigated the effectiveness of a training program for novice teaching assistants (TAs) as measured by the achievement of undergraduate students of the assistants. Eight TAs were trained in the use of certain lower-inference teacher behaviors through the use of protocol videotapes and microteaching experiences. Each TA was matched on cultural background and spoken English ability with an untrained TA. Where extraneous variables did not violate the research design, significant differences were found in student achievement in favor of the trained foreign TAs. While all TAs demonstrated a cognitive assimilation of the behaviors in the training program, this assimilation was uniformly translated into performance in the classroom. The use of certain behaviors was found to be related to the interaction between training and spoken-English ability. It was found that trained American TAs included in the study performed certain behaviors significantly more than the foreign TAs or untrained American TAs. The observation instrument developed for this study is fully described and indices of validity and reliability provided. An extinguishing effect of the behaviors was detected over the six-week period of classroom observation of the TA performance. Findings suggested that cultural background and/or spoken English ability may inhibit the practice of learned behaviors in the classroom situation. In the given recitation situation, the use of certain behaviors may be inappropriate. The use of behaviors by the TAs tended to be extinguished over time, suggesting that some form of reinforcement is essential if learned behaviors are to be practiced. Questions discussed for further research included the impact of training on the TAs in other than intended areas of impact; the type of behaviors appropriate for a given level of recitation section; the impact of TA background culture and spoken English ability upon TA potential for training and ability to make use of the training in the classroom; and the effect on undergraduate students in the classroom in terms of compensatory behaviors when confronted by a TA who experiences difficulty in communicating. A comprehensive review of the literature related to TA training is provided.

Gburek, Janice L. and Dunnett, Stephen C., eds. *The Foreign TA: A Guide to Teaching Effectiveness.* Buffalo, NY: State University of New York at Buffalo, 1986. 59 p.

A collection of articles submitted by experienced foreign and American TAs and by undergraduates who have been taught by TAs, this volume provides information, suggestions, and encouragement to foreign TAs who are about to undertake teaching responsibilities at SUNY-Buffalo. Questions discussed include adaptation to U.S. academic environment, the role of TA, undergraduate expectations, communication skills, gaining confidence, teaching of a laboratory class, teaching of recitation class, and places to get help. Background information of U.S. higher education system is provided at the beginning.

Articles

Ard, Josh. "The Foreign TA Problem from an Acquisition-Theoretic Point of View". *English for Specific Purposes* 6, No. 2 (1987): 133-144.

Relates research on second-language acquisition and research on the language problems of foreign teaching assistants and their remediation. On the one hand, second-language-acquisition findings could improve the specific instructional programs required for foreign teaching assistants. On the other hand, second-language-acquisition research has not addressed specific data of this type. Argues that several vogue models of second-language-acquisition cannot explain the specific data without amendments. In particular, the psychological construct of attention is an important factor in determining whether or not the specific language use expected of college teachers will be attained by foreign students.

Braxton, John M. and Nordall, Robert C. "Colleges Try Tests and Training to Make Sure Foreign TA's Can Be Understood". *Chronicle of Higher Education* (September 11, 1985): 32-33.

Constantinides, Janet C. "The 'Foreign TA Problem' -- An Update". *NAFSA Newsletter* 38 (March, 1987): 3-6.

Fisher, Michele. "Rethinking the 'Foreign TA Problem'". *New Directions for Teaching and Learning (Strengthening the Teaching Assistant Faculty)* No. 22 (June, 1985): 63-73.

The article discusses the cultural and language barriers facing foreign teaching assistants. It then suggests that universities may test the spoken English ability of foreign graduate students and train currently employed foreign teaching assistants through lectures, tapes, and demonstration of teaching skills; information on American campus life; and English practice.

Lulat, Y. G-M. and Weiler, J. "Teaching Competency of Foreign TAs Does Not Rest on Language Alone". In *The Foreign TA: A Guide to Teaching Effectiveness*, eds. J. Gburek and S. Dunnett (Buffalo, NY: Intensive English Language Institute, State University of New York at Buffalo, 1986): 13-15.

McMillen, Liz. "Teaching Assistants Get Increased Training". *Chronicle of Higher Education* (October 29, 1986): 9-11.

Rice, Donna Steed. "A One Semester Program for Orienting the New Foreign Teaching Assistant". In *Foreign Teaching Assistants in U.S. Universities*, eds. K. Bailey, et al. (Washington, D.C.: National Association of Foreign Student Affairs, 1984): 69-75.

20. Attitudinal and Behavioral Studies

Books

Geuer, Wolfgang; Breitenbach, Diether, and Dadder, Rita. *Psychische Probleme auslandischer Studenten in der BRD. Bericht uber eine Studie im Auftrag des DAAD. (Psychological Problems of Foreign Students in the FRG. A Report of a Study Commissioned by the German Academic Exchange Service).* Saarbrucken: Universitat des Saarlandes, Fachrichtung Psychologie, 1983. 199 p.

> This study of 500 institutions that provide for the care and advisement of foreign students and practitioners inquired into their experiences with the treatment of psychological problems of foreigners. The results of the questionnaire provide an overview of the social and medical services available to foreign students in the FRG. According to the interviewees, the most widespread problems are work and achievement pressures, examination anxiety, and problems of self-worth and identity.

Goodwin, Crauford and Nacht, Michael. *Fondness and Frustration: The Impact of American Higher Education on Foreign Students with Special Reference to the Case of Brazil.* New York: Institute of International Education, 1984.

> This study of Brazilian graduates of American universities who had returned to Brazil focuses on such questions as the impressions of the graduates concerning American higher education, reentry issues, curricular questions, and others. Among the findings are:
>
> • Virtually all of the respondents reported that they had learned a great deal in the United States and had a positive impression of their education.

• However, the authors emphasize the importance of careful selection of students and careful placement in order to minimize problems.

• There is a serious possibility of a mismatch between students and institutions, since American higher education is large and complex.

• It was emphasized that in order to keep up the skills of the graduates it is important to maintain contact with them, perhaps through the American universities from which they graduated.

• Agencies that are funding and providing education for Brazilian students need to coordinate activities and to pay much closer attention to the kind of education being imparted. These agencies include U.S. government departments, colleges and universities, international organizations, and multinational corporations.

• Students reported that the education that they received in the U.S. was not always what was expected, but frequently they found it useful and stimulating.

• Reentry problems were frequent, particularly since practices in Brazil did not relate to the content and orientation of the education received in the U.S.

• Graduate students in the social sciences and humanities felt that their American educational experience was very positive. They did not find the materials or curriculum surprising and felt that immersion in the culture of American graduate education was particularly valuable.

LeCastre, Richard J. *Foreign Student Attitude Formation Toward the United States.* Ph.D. Dissertation, State University of New York at Buffalo, 1987. 312 p. Order No. DA8718548

This study attempts to gain insight into the dynamics underlying regard directed toward the host country for foreign students studying in the United States. Through the analysis of survey data and relevant student comment, a better understanding of the choice process surrounding the foreign student decision to come to the U.S. for study and whether or not to remain in the U.S. following that study is sought. A central issue is how and why attitudes change toward the U.S. during the course of the educational sojourn abroad for a randomly selected sample of 580 students studying at three higher educational institutions in the State University of New York (SUNY) system (334 responded).

Some of the major findings include: (1) The SUNY student characteristics and demographic profiles parallel national data. (2) Composite attitude indices measuring student regard toward host and home countries reveal a complex mixture of positive and negative elements. (3) Students late in the sojourn report U.S. attitudes that remain the same (41%), improve (31%), or worsen (28%) since first arrival. (4) Improved U.S. regard tends to be associated with decisions to stay. (5) Most students (64%) express a desire to remain temporarily in the U.S. following completion of studies (7% would stay permanently, 29% return home). (6) No support for the reputed U-curve hypothesis is found. (7) Analysis of student comments coalesce into certain themes reflecting stereotypes of America/Americans (e.g., tolerant/friendly Americans caught up in an evil government; Americans as self-starving, superficial, and materialistic; the commercialization of television as reflected in the selling of products and ideology). (8) Despite critical reservations, evidence supports the contention that regard toward the U.S. is more positive than negative.

Theoretical arguments using a Cognitive Dissonance Model are offered to suggest that push/pull factors are not only associated with transnational student flows but also with attitude-formation toward the host country. A direct relationship between maintenance of positive regard toward the host country and the perceived degree of influence of push/pull factors on returning students is postulated.

Liu, Yi-Rong Young. *Chinese Intellectuals' Sense of Mission and Their Attitude Toward Foreign Study.* Ph.D. Dissertation, University of California, Los Angeles, 1985. 240 p. Order No. DA8525891

Foreign study is one of the most important events in modern China's educational development. In the past century, more than two hundred thousand Chinese students studied abroad. Most of the students going abroad before 1949 returned to China with a patriotic drive to serve the nation and made great contributions to China's modernization. In the recent years, however, the brain-drain problem has characterized Taiwan's foreign education. It is observed that an attitude change has occurred among the recent Chinese intellectuals.

This study examined the Chinese students' changing attitude toward foreign study and its relation with the sense of mission. Both historical and empirical methods were adopted. Through a historical review, it was found that the early Chinese students' attitude toward foreign study was greatly influenced by their sense of mission. They went abroad mainly for the purpose of acquiring Western technology and serving their mother country. They actively participated in patriotic movements and political activities.

This study also presented statistical comparisons between the early students and the recent ones in their (1) field of study, (2) occupational distribution, and (3) returning rate. Statistical comparisons and other empirical findings showed that the recent students were more concerned with personal interests (salary and job opportunity) when selecting their fields of study. They were more devoted to high-reward sectors (business and industry) in the occupational comparison with the early students. Their returning rate was much lower than that of the early students. All these findings indicated an attitude change and a decrease of the sense of mission among the recent students.

The findings from interviews with the foreign-educated Taiwanese intellectuals supported the historical study and the statistical comparisons. They also revealed that economic and political factors were major contributors to the self-interest orientation of the recent students. This study suggested that self-actualization instead of political commitment may be the new mission for today's Taiwanese intellectuals.

Rizk, Ali Abdul Hassan. *A Study of Communication Patterns of International Students in the Process of Acculturation.* Ph.D. Dissertation, Ohio University, 1986.

Salem, Elia Awwad. *Attitudes of International Students from Developing Countries Toward Campus Professional Psychological Services.* Ph.D. Dissertation, Southern Illinois University at Carbondale, 1985.

Articles

Abdalla, Saleh E. and Gibson, Janice T. "The Relationship of Exposure to American Culture on the Attitude of Libyan Nationals Toward the Role of Women in the Workforce". *Contemporary Educational Psychology* 9 (July, 1984): 294-302.

The article explores whether Libyan nationals who have stayed in the United States for long periods of time and who have had more exposure to American attitudes and values express more "modern" attitudes toward the role of women in the workforce than Libyan nationals who have been in the U.S. for shorter periods. It finds that there is no relationship between the length of stay in the U.S. and the attitude scores of the subjects in the study. However, the study reveals that the higher the educational level of the females, the more likely they are going to express "modern" attitudes toward women in the workforce. Therefore, it concludes that increase in educational opportunities currently being made available in Libya together with opportunities for more and more women to travel abroad and to gain exposure to other more "modern" cultures may well be related to major changes in attitudes of females in the future.

Adebayo, Akin and Nassif, Fatima. "Options Regarding Abortion Among Male Nigerian Undergraduate Students in the United States". *Social Biology* 32 (Spring, 1985): 132-135.

Adebayo, A. "Shifting Fertility Attitudes of Nigerian Students by Duration of Stay in the United States". *Sociology and Social Research* 70 (July, 1986): 284-285.

Cummings, William K. and So, W. C. "The Preference of Asian Overseas Students for the United States: An Examination of the Context". *Higher Education* 14 (August, 1985): 403-423.

The article discusses numerous factors in Asian students' choice of U.S. study, which include improved political relations, increased Asian-American exchange, increased Asian immigration to the U.S., similarity in educational structure and content, the absorptive capacity and quality of American higher education, complementarity of supply and demand, and opportunities for financial self-help.

Cummings, William K. "Why Asian Overseas Students Prefer the United States". In *Higher Education Expansion in Asia*. Hiroshima, Japan: Research Institute for Higher Education, 1985: 118-140.

Demmellash, T. "On Marxism and Ethiopian Student Radicalism in North America". *Monthly Review* 35 (February, 1984): 25-37.

Furnham, A. and Albihai, N. "Value Differences in Foreign Students". *International Journal of Intercultural Relations* 9, No. 4 (1985): 365-375.

The Rokeach Value Survey was administered to four equivalent groups of students studying in London. It was hypothesized that a number of differences would occur between these groups based on their country of origin, respective affluence, and traditional cultural values. The study found that half of the values showed significant differences between groups, with the British control group and the Europeans being most often more similar to each other than the other groups. The Africans were most different from the three other groups. These results were attributed to the cultural and economic differences and related specifically to the literature of sojourner adjustment.

Hojat, Mohammadreza; Shapurian, Reza, and Mehryar, Amir H. "Psychometric Properties of a Persian Version of the Short Form of the Beck Depression Inventory for Iranian College Students". *Psychological Reports* 59 (August, 1986): 331-338.

The psychometric properties of the short form of the Beck Depression Inventory were studied in two Iranian groups. The inventory was translated into Persian, and 12 bilingual Iranian judges confirmed the soundness of the translation. The sample comprised two groups of Iranian college students; data were analyzed separately for each group. Group I consisted of 232 Iranian students who were studying in American universities, and Group II consisted of 305 Iranian students studying in Iranian universities. Descriptive statistics and test-retest reliability were reported. Significantly positive correlations between the scores of depression inventory and measures of anxiety, loneliness, and externality of locus of control were found. Negative correlations were also obtained. The results provided evidence that supported the validity and reliability of the depression inventory in Iranian college students.

Horsley, Doyne A. "A Comparison of American and Non-American Students' Attitudes on Issues of the Physical Environment". *Journal of Environmental Education* 15 (Spring, 1984): 37-42.

Attitudes of students in three American high school classes were compared to attitudes of students in ten foreign schools. Results indicate that American students varied considerably among the three schools but overall rated the environment more positively than did foreign students.

Lee, M. Y. "Judgements of Significant Others and Self-Concept of Students from Developing Nations". *Journal of Social Psychology* 122 (February, 1984): 127-134.

Examines three views of self-concept as perceived by students from developing countries at selected U.S. universities with regard to their academic performance, their intelligence, and their physical appearance: that held by friends in their home countries as perceived by the students (one set of significant others); that held by U.S. students as perceived by the students (another set of significant others); and that held by the students themselves. Finds that in all three aspects of self, the students perceived the image of themselves held by friends in their home countries as highest, that held by U.S. students as lowest, and that held by themselves ranking between the two. Also found are the additional variations in their perception of self-concept in terms of their student classification, sponsorship, sex, and country of origin.

Lee, M. Y. "Prestige of Home Country and Self-Concept of Students from Four Developing Countries". *Journal of Social Psychology* 126 (August, 1986): 485-491.

Three views of prestige of home countries as perceived by students from Iran, Nigeria, Taiwan, and Venezuela were examined in relation to the students' perceptions of their academic performance, their intelligence, and their physical appearance. The three views of a country's prestige were perceptions of views held by students in the U.S.A.; perceptions of views held by friends in their home country; and the perceptions of the students themselves. Overall, the prestige ratings were most strongly correlated with the students' own physical-appearance ratings and then with their intelligence ratings. Variations of correlations by view and by country were also found.

Leong, F. T. L. and Sedlacek, W. E. "A Comparison of International and United States Students' Preferences for Help Sources". *Journal of College Student Personnel* 27 (September, 1986): 426-430.

International students were more likely than students from the United States to prefer faculty members and counselors and less likely to prefer friends for help with all kinds of problems.

Manese, J. E.; Leong, W. E., and Sedlacek, W. E. "Background, Attitudes and Needs of Undergraduate International Students". *College Student Affairs Journal* No. 6 (Spring, 1985): 19-28.

At the University of Maryland in fall 1982, all 96 incoming undergraduate international students completed at orientation a questionnaire on their background, perceptions, goals, attitudes, and lifestyles. The responses indicated that annual family income for international students ranged from less than $5,000 to over $50,000, with only 21% of the students expected to earn their own tuition. Sixty-nine percent of the students had been in the U.S. for at least two years. In general, the students had good academic records, 68% indicating that they had graduated in the top 1/4 of their secondary school class. As for purpose of study, 37% viewed college a place to prepare for a career, while 37% saw it as most important for pursuit of knowledge. They were most concerned with exploring job opportunities. They most expected to need help in selecting and scheduling classes and developing study/writing skills.

Murase, A. E. "High Education and Lifestyle Aspirations of Japanese and Nonreturnee Students". *Bulletin of the Faculty of Foreign Studies* (Sophia University, Japan), (March, 1985).

Okigbo, C. "Media Use by Foreign Students". *Journalism Quarterly* 62, No. 4 (1985): 901-904.

Sell, Deborah K. "Research on Attitude Change in U.S. Students Who Participate in Foreign Study Experiences: Past Findings and Suggestions for Future Research". *International Journal of Inter-Cultural Relations* 7, No. 2 (1983): 131-147.

Includes five studies utilizing one-time questioning of program participants and fifteen articles employing analysis of pre- and post-sojourn questionnaires. Finds that attitude change is seldom verified empirically in these works and attributes this phenomenon to loosely structured experimental designs, infrequent use of follow-up studies, lack of an established theoretical base, and perhaps most importantly, and lack of a consensus concerning what to measure. Suggests that future research should include the study of specific variables thought to facilitate attitude change, analysis of subgroups of students similar on a particular characteristic or ability, and measurement of behavioral competencies.

Sharma, M. P. and Klasek, C. B. "Does the Involvement of American Institutions of Higher Education in International Programs Abroad Affect the International Attitudes of American Students?" *Journal of Studies in Technical Careers* 8 (Fall, 1986): 295-306.

Stohl, Cynthia. "The A.M.I.G.O. Project: A Multicultural Intergroup Opportunity". *International Journal of Intercultural Relations* 9, No. 2 (1985): 151-175.

Describes and analyzes an empirical investigation of significant attitudinal changes incurred as a result of participation in a semester-long intercultural experience. Finds that students became more accepting of diversity and differences, felt greater responsibility to and increased importance of foreign visitors to the United States, and developed a sense of importance and desire for travel abroad. Discusses both the implications and the limitations of the study.

21. Cross-Cultural Issues and Activities

Books

Baldassare, Mark and Katz, Cheryl. *International Exchange Off-Campus: Foreign Students and Local Communities.* New York: Institute of International Education, 1987. 44 p.

The focus of this empirical study is on the impact of foreign students on local communities. A town of 33,000 in the northeast United States with one large university and a small college were chosen for the research site. Through the use of questionnaires and interviews, the following key findings developed:

1. Fewer than one in three foreign students surveyed knew "a lot" or "some" town residents by name, although most perceived residents as "friendly".

2. More than half of the foreign students did not recollect either pleasant or unpleasant encounters with townspeople.

3. Foreign students with town contacts were no more likely than others to wish to remain in the U.S. after study.

4. Townspeople were generally unaware of the presence of foreign students. The majority of contacts were business-related, and these were quite casual. A group of about 100 townspeople participate more in home visits, etc.

5. Most foreign students place little value on town encounters.

6. Most town residents place little value on foreign student encounters.

Behringer, Gerhard. *Untersuchung des Zusammenhangs Zwischen interkulturellen Erfahrungen und Einstellung zur internationalen Zusammenarbeit am Beispiel des Auslandsstudiums in den U.S.A. (An Examination of the Relationship Between Intercultural Experiences and Attitudes Toward International Cooperation: Foreign Study in the U.S.A.).* Regensburg: Universitat Regensburg, Lehrstuhl Sozial-Psychologie, 1983. 184 p.

This "Diplom" thesis is based on a study of 27 German students who studied in the United States in 1982. They were interviewed before, during, and after their study-abroad experience in order to collect data about their interactions and contacts, level of overall satisfaction, and the broadening of their experiential horizons. The results show that the readiness for international cooperation increased whereby those with highly positive attitudes were sobered somewhat by their experience. The question remains whether these documented changes in attitude will remain intact and to what extent they are linked to personality characteristics or dependent upon certain situations in the foreign country. These issues must be resolved before the political effects of international student exchange can be ascertained.

Byrd, Patricia, ed. *Teaching Across Cultures in the University ESL Program*. Washington, D.C.: National Association for Foreign Student Affairs, 1986.

This volume deals with the issues raised by the conflict of one cultural group with another within an ESL program on a college or university campus. Three topics are covered: (1) background discussion of the relevant issues; (2) programs developed at the institutional or program level; and (3) materials and methods developed by individual teachers. Section I addresses the general and theoretical aspect of the first topic; Section II describes the cross-cultural communication and orientation programs developed by four institutions; and Section III discusses materials and courses individual teachers have developed in response to various needs they have found among their students. An annotated bibliography is provided.

Campbell, Jean Baird. *Cultural Contact As University International Students Provide Service in American Schools and Communities*. Ph.D. Dissertation, University of Oregon, 1987. 302 p. Order No. DA8721229

This study describes and analyzes a program designed to address issues of effective teaching and learning about other cultural groups. University of Oregon international students in the International Cultural Service Program received financial aid in exchange for "cultural service" in schools, in the community, and at the university. Program participants interacted with Americans of all ages as they spoke about their countries or shared language and cultural knowledge in educational, social, and business settings. In the ethnically homogeneous county where the study was conducted, the program provided an opportunity for local citizens to meet individuals from other countries and cultural groups.

Observations in schools led to descriptions of program use, content of the presentations, and student questions at different educational levels. Teachers believed that the unique program feature was the direct cultural contact, which contributed to students' global interest and understanding of cultural differences and similarities. Interviews with second, seventh, and ninth graders suggested cognitive and affective dimensions of the interaction. Student responses were interpreted according to developmental models, indicating that awareness preceded understanding of different perspectives. The study was related to other research on global education, stereotypic thinking, ethnocentrism, social studies, and anthropology.

Cultural contact through the program generally was positive because of shared goals, mutual respect, and a discourse of "politeness" in which participants behaved as good guests and hosts. The university recruited and retained well-qualified international students. The community gained otherwise unavailable services and global perspectives. School students received "insider" views of other cultures and developed tolerance for "difference". The international students received financial assistance and increased their public speaking skills, national pride, and understanding of American culture. Their cultural identity was affected as they responded to stereotypes and assessed attitude and behavior changes through immersion in the host society.

Cousins, Joseph M. *The Effects of Cross-Cultural Training on American Students in Their Interaction with Foreign Students in an International House.* Unpublished Ph.D. Dissertation, Kansas State University, 1984. 99 p. Order No. DA8427879

The purpose of this study was to determine if cross-cultural-communication training produces more changes in the interaction toward foreign students by American students than occurs by just residing in an international house.

From the results of statistical analysis, the following conclusions were drawn: (1) There was evidence that randomization occurred when assigning subjects to treatment and control groups. (2) There was no statistical evidence that cross-cultural-communication training will increase the interaction of American students toward their foreign peers. (3) Evidence indicated that over time, the interaction between American and foreign students did change, but that the interaction in fact decreased while living in an international environment. (4) There was no significant interaction found between combinations of groups, pre-testing, and time.

Furnham, Adrian and Bochner, S. *Culture Shock: Psychological Reactions to Unfamiliar Environment.* London: Methuen, 1986.

This book does not deal exclusively with foreign students, but has direct relevance to the study of foreign-student-adjustment issues and problems. By looking at different studies of cultural adjustment among people in non-native environments, the authors ask a variety of questions concerning adjustment and "culture shock". Among the groups looked at are political refugees, foreign students, business travellers, and tourists in settings in Australia, Britain, Canada, Germany, and the United States. Questions such as how can culture shock be alleviated and are migrants more distressed than tourists are asked. Chapters deal with such topics as the psychology of intercultural contact, the varieties of cultural travellers, coping with unfamiliar environments, and culture learning and management. A comprehensive bibliography is included.

Kobrin, S. J. *International Expertise in American Business.* New York: Institute of International Education, 1984. 59 p.

This report focuses on the international competence of American business leaders. It deals with the attitudes of businessmen concerning international expertise, language ability of business leaders, the acquiring of international expertise, and related issues. The implications for international education are also discussed.

Najafi, Vahid. *MMPI Personality Dimensions and Levels of Assertiveness in Iranian and American College Students.* Unpublished Ph.D. Dissertation, St. John's University, 1985.   99 p. Order No. DA8508817

Cross-cultural and longitudinal comparisons were made between 40 Iranian and 40 American students attending several northeastern universities. Differences in personality and levels of assertiveness were determined by administering the Minnesota Multiphasic Personality Inventory and Rathus Assertiveness Schedule to all subjects.   Iranians obtained significantly higher scores than Americans on the L, F, D, Pt, Sc and Si standard scales and A, Lb, Ca, and Pr special scales of the MMPI.   In contrast, Americans scored significantly higher than Iranians on the Es and St special scales.

Longitudinal evaluation involved a smaller sample of students due to subject attrition between pre- and post-test assessment. However, Iranian post-test MMPI profiles were more similar to American MMPI profiles.   This suggested that certain personality dimensions were influenced by situational factors. However, other dimensions remained more resistant to change, suggesting the role of cultural factors in personality development.

On the Rathus Assertiveness Schedule, American students scored significantly higher on assertiveness than Iranian students. These results were compatible with data obtained on the MMPI, indicating that Americans were more extroverted than Iranians. The findings in this study have several implications with respect to the formulation of effective counseling strategies for foreign students, and illuminate certain personality differences that may impede the communication process between counselor and student.

Paige, R. Michael. *Cross-Cultural Orientation: New Conceptions and Applications.* Lanham, MD: University Press of America, 1985.

Sami, Mohammad Bagher. *A Model for Orientation Program of Adjustment of Foreign Students in American Colleges and Universities.* Ph.D. Dissertation, George Peabody College for Teachers of Vanderbilt University, 1986. 162 p. Order No. DA8619640

The survey questionnaire for this cross-cultural study was distributed to 340 international students from 48 countries enrolled in public institutions of higher education in the state of Tennessee. The questionnaire and its scales attempted to answer questions related to needs of foreign students for orientation and how much more assistance home countries and American colleges and universities should provide to international students in early adjustment to the new academic/social environment. The purpose of the study was to determine the nature and components of existing orientation programs for foreign students related to their life/study in the United States, the benefits of these programs as perceived by the participants, and suggestions on improvement of such programs.

The findings indicate: (a) the majority of participants (with or without orientation) thought orientation played an important role in academic success and social/cultural adjustment; (b) the degree of importance for those who had orientation was much stronger; (c) the need of orientation was related to cultural and regional background of students; and (d) the present orientation programs are not adequate and do not meet the needs of international students and more comprehensive orientation programs are needed. Age, degree, length of time in U.S., sex, and spouse had no effect on participant's view of the importance of orientation.

Shankar, Archana Daya. *A Descriptive Study: An Examination of International University Students' Problems, Support Networks and Communication Issues.* Ph.D. Dissertation, Ohio University, 1987. 170 p. Order No. DA8719363

Communication is one of the areas in which international students face serious problems. This study attempts to examine problems in communication experienced by international students in American universities.

Questionnaires were administered to the international students attending four different American universities: Ohio University, Athens, Ohio; Marshall University, Huntington, WV; Central Missouri State University, Warrensburg, MO; and the University of Washington, Seattle, WA.

The results suggest that length of stay in the United States does minimize the students' problems in the area of communication. The longer they stay in the United States the less problems students face. Compared with males, females experience more fear of speaking in classrooms.

The majority of the students go mainly to two support groups: their professors and/or to the students who come from their own countries. Very few students go to their family members, the host families, or to the ombudsman. Very few female students seek support from the office of international students. Male students seem to use this office more often.

Articles

Bochner, S., et al. "The Friendship Patterns of Overseas and Host Students in an Oxford Student Residence". *Journal of Social Psychology* 125 (December, 1985): 689-694.

By asking twenty-three overseas and nine English residents at an Oxford student residence to name their three best friends in England, this study finds that only 17% of the friends of foreign students were English, and only 26% of the friends of English students were foreign. It concludes that the results of this study are consistent with previous findings that international houses are not overly successful in facilitating the creation of bonds between foreign students and host nationals.

Bulthuis, Jill D. "The Foreign Student Today: A Profile". In *Guiding the Development of Foreign Students*, ed. K. Pyle (San Francisco: Jossey-Bass, 1986): 19-28.

This chapter responds to such questions as "Who are foreign students", "What are their attitudes, needs, and concerns", and "What are the special issues they face that we need to be aware of". It points out that a better understanding of foreign students is critical if we are to be effective facilitators of foreign students' growth and development. It concludes that sensitivity to different cultural expectations concerning classroom behavior, appropriate roles of faculty and staff, and the way services should be provided may alleviate misunderstanding and frustration for all involved.

Camilleri, C. "Les étudiants étrangers en France et leur discours sur l'identité culturelle". *Bulletin de Psychologie* 37, No. 364 (1984): 287-297.

This article reports on a study carried out at the Université Rene Descartes (Paris) in 1978 and 1979. The sample consisted of 100 foreign students enrolled in psychology. The study finds:

1. The female students referred to "identity" in reference to their families, ethnic groups, or minority groups, while the male students conceived "identity" beyond the national boundaries. The study also found that students from Black Africa were more attached to an "African culture" dealing with the continent as a whole rather than individual identity. As to when cultural identity takes place, the study suggests two main groups of responses: (1) those who responded that they became aware of their identity as a result of individual maturation; i.e., reflection on the topic (0.36), studies (0.16), and individual political maturation (0.10); and (2) those who asserted that they became conscious of their cultural identity as a result of external factors (0.50), and political actions (0.16).

2. With regard to the means of keeping one's identity, 50 percent of the sample suggested that it could be done by preserving the

traditional values. About one third of the sample responded that political means were necessary. In total, more males than females, 0.36 and 0.23 respectively, suggested political means. Other responses include grouping students from the same countries together and comparing different cultures. When asked if the survival of the cultural identity was tied to the survival of national languages, half of the sample responded yes.

3. Ninety percent of the sample suggested that Western culture was still attempting to dominate other cultures. According to them, Western culture is a colonial tool. The responses also suggested that education, the transmission of knowledge, was a means of cultural domination (0.43).

4. For more than a third of the sample, (36%), there is no contradiction between identity and change. However, 9% reject change, since it might affect their identity. A large proportion of the sample (56%) was embarrassed by the question and did not respond.

5. More than half of the students interviewed reported that their stay in France has changed their initial ideas about France's culture. Eight percent have experienced a "cultural shock", and a quarter of the sample reported not having been affected by their stay in France. Change and cultural shock have been more experienced by females than by males (62% and 47% respectively). More importantly, students from Black Africa (80%) reported having been shocked by the "distant attitude" of French people.

Cousins, Joseph. "The Effects of Cross-Cultural Training on American Students in an International House". *Journal of International Student Personnel* 2, No. 3 (1985): 20-24.

DeCarbo, Edward. "Diversity and the International Community: Mobilizing Resources". *Campus Activities Programming* 19 (April, 1987): 51-55.

Furnham, A. and Alibhai, N. "The Friendship Networks of Foreign
Students: A Replication and Extension of the Functional Model".
International Journal of Psychology 20, No. 6 (1985): 709-722.

> The purpose of this study was to replicate and extend the study
> by Bochner et al. (1977) that presented a functional model for the
> development of overseas-student friendship patterns. While
> Bochner et al. used only 30 Far Eastern foreign students and six
> host nationals in his Hawaian study, Furnham and Alibhai used
> 140 foreign students from each continent. The subjects in this
> study were asked to specify various aspects of their three best
> friends and their preferred companion for each of a range of
> everyday situations. The data on friendship network showed a
> strong preference for co-national friends first, other nationals
> second, and host nationals third, while the data on preferred
> companion revealed co-nationals first, then host nationals, and
> finally "other" nationals. The results of this study match those
> of Bochner et al. (1977) and provide further evidence for the
> functional model.

Furnham, Adrian and Bochner, S. "Social Difficulty in a Foreign
Culture: An Empirical Analysis of Culture Shock". In *Cultures in
Contact*, ed. S. Bochner (New York: Pergamon, 1982): 161-198.

Grubbs, Lisa L. "Multicultural Training in University Residence
Halls". *Journal of College and University Student Housing* 15
(Winter, 1985): 21-25.

Gudykunst, William B. "An Exploratory Comparison of Close
Intracultural and Intercultural Friendships". *Communication
Quarterly* 33 (Fall, 1985): 270-283.

> Data from two studies suggest: (1) people who make friends in
> their home culture also tend to make friends while in another
> culture, and (2) close intracultural and intercultural
> relationships have analogous patterns.

Hara, Katsuko. "My One-Year Stay in Arizona". *Biblos* 37, No. 11
(1986): 17-25.

Horowitz, Ruth Tamar T., and Kraus, Vered. "Patterns of Cultural Transition: Soviet and American Children in a New Environment". *Journal of Cross-Cultural Psychology* 15 (December, 1984): 399-416.

A comparative study of the adjustment of immigrant students from the USSR and North America to the Israeli education system, revealing distinct differences between the two groups. The differences between the social environment in the countries of origin were hypothesized to affect the pattern of adjustment both in school and society at large. Students from North America were found to be age-group oriented, whereas students from the USSR are adult oriented and place strong emphasis on the student-teacher relationship.

Nichols, Keith R. and McAndrew, Francis T. "Stereotyping and Autostereotyping in Spanish, Malaysian, and American College Students". *Journal of Social Psychology* 124 (December, 1984): 179-189.

Examines the stereotypes among groups of college students, including the Spanish, Malaysians, and Americans, in terms of the amount of contact each subject group had had with each of the stimulus cultures. Reveals significant differences in the content of the stereotypes held by each of these groups as well as distinct tendencies to see others in a particular way. Autostereotypes are found to be as variable as stereotypes. The amount of contact with another culture strongly influences both.

Sadow, S. A. "Experiential Techniques that Promote Cross-Cultural Awareness". *Foreign Language Annals* 20 (February, 1987): 25-30.

Sharma, M. P. and Jung, L. B. "How Cross-Cultural Social Participation Affects the International Attitudes of United States Students". *International Journal of Intercultural Relations* 9, No. 4 (1985): 377-387.

Investigates the impact of U.S. students' interaction with international students on the concept of cosmopolitan world outlook, cultural pluralism, world-mindedness, understanding of own culture, support for internationalism, international career aspirations, and political liberalism. Finds that interaction between student cultures does facilitate and encourage an international outlook. Points out that institutes should strive to promote activities that will encourage and maintain a high degree of cultural interactions between U.S. and international students.

"Ways of Learning from International Students". *Intercom* No. 106 (1985): 39-42.

Wilson, Angene H. "Exchange Students As Bridges Between Cultures". *Intercom* No. 106 (March, 1985): 5-8.

The article discusses the benefits of encouraging returned American exchange students and foreign exchange students to be bridges between cultures. It then examines obstacles in the way of exchange students being utilized as resources. A scenario describing how a social studies teacher could encourage exchange students to increase cross-cultural awareness is also introduced.

22. Curricular Issues and Programs of Study

Books

Jenkins, Hugh M. *Strategies for Professional Integration: Strengthening Foreign Student/Private Sector Interaction -- A Report of a Seminar.* Washington, D.C.: National Association for Foreign Student Affairs, 1985. 12 p.

NAFSA Consulting Team. *The ARAMCO Industrial Training Centers: Academic Training and College Preparatory Programs.* Washington, D.C.: National Association for Foreign Student Affairs, May, 1985. 31 p.

Programs for Spouses of Foreign Students. Washington, D.C.:
National Association for Foreign Student Affairs, 1986. 25 p.

> Deals with design of programs that cater to the increasing
> number of foreign students' spouses and other family members.
> The problems and needs of foreign spouses are analyzed in
> comparison to those of foreign students. Aspects of programs
> discussed include club activities, instruction, health care classes,
> professional contacts, coordinating activities, child care,
> sponsorship, budget, facilities, meeting schedules, needs
> assessment, and evaluation. Samples of brochure, invitation,
> information card, evaluation form, and newsletter are included
> in the appendices.

Vozzella, Robert Eugene. *A Model for the Implementation of a
Cooperative Education Program Involving Foreign Students.* Ed.D.
Dissertation, Northeastern University, 1987.

Wakim, Agnes Melhem. *The Relevance of U.S. University Programs
in Education to Needs and Goals of International Graduate Students
from Developing Countries.* Ed.D. Dissertation, Boston University,
1985.

Articles

Brod, Evelyn F. "The Amity Scholar Program in Two-Year
Colleges". *Hispanic* 70 (March, 1987): 177-180.

Cashman, Kristin and Plihal, Jane. "International Agriculture
Students' Perceptions of the Relevance of Their U.S. Education".
Journal of Agronomic Education 16 (Fall, 1987): 61-65.

> Recent studies indicate that 25% of all graduate students
> studying agriculture in the U.S. are from less developed
> countries. Previous studies on the relevance of U.S. education
> provided to international agriculture students have relied on
> written surveys with predetermined and standardized categories
> and have stopped short of offering specific recommendations for
> increasing the relevance of such education. This study explores

the extent to which U.S. land-grant universities provide experiences to help foreign students in approaching agricultural problems in less developed countries. Open-ended interviews are made to 28 international agriculture students at the University of Minnesota. Presents the findings concerning students' agricultural backgrounds, agricultural situations in students' home countries, and students' impressions of U.S. education. Two recommendations are made for making U.S. education more relevant for foreign agricultural students: (1) include field experiences in students' study programs; (2) refocus the direction and approach of research conducted by international agriculture students.

"Classroom Activities -- Using International Students As Resources". *Intercom* No. 106 (1985): 12-38.

This section contains five classroom-ready sample lessons demonstrating how international students can be used as resources in the secondary social-studies classroom. Included are lessons showing how they can contribute to courses such as U.S. history and how they can become involved in various classroom activities. It also illustrates how their involvement can serve to develop and strengthen the skills, attitudes, and content areas covered in standard secondary social-studies curriculum. The lessons are followed by a list of ideas for using international students as resources in social studies classes at elementary and secondary level.

Cope, Johnnye and Black, Evelyn. "New Library Orientation for International Students". *College Teaching* 33 (Fall, 1985): 159-162.

Fox, John and Mutangira, Joseph. "The Overseas Training of Adult Educators: An Evaluation of Programs in Africa and the U.K.; Some Emerging Themes". *International Journal of Educational Development* 5, No. 2 (1985): 241-244.

Goudy, Frank W. and Moushey, Eugene. "Library Instruction and Foreign Students: A Survey of Opinions and Practices Among Selected Libraries". *Reference Librarian* 10 (Spring/Summer, 1984): 215-226.

Reports a survey of 44 academic libraries on opinions and practices related to library services to foreign students. Survey objectives include: perceived adequacy of library skills possessed by foreign students as compared to native-born students; the helpfulness of library instruction to foreign students; existing library-instruction programs already being implemented; coordination existing between the library and other related components of the university. Findings include: (1) lack of familiarity with available resources is more severe with foreign students; (2) library orientation tends to be most prevalent form of instruction; (3) two-thirds of the libraries are involved in collaborating efforts. Suggests that a specific program of library instruction is needed to overcome the difficulties of foreign students in using library resources. Provides sources of additional ideas and programs for services to foreign students.

Greenfield, Louise, et al. "Educating the World: Training Library Staff to Communicate Effectively with International Students". *Journal of Academic Librarianship* 12 (September, 1986): 227-231.

The article describes a workshop developed by the University of Arizona Library to train its staff in cross-cultural communication, including its rationale, goals, and content of the session. Concerns addressed include language difficulties, cultural adjustment, and library instruction for international students.

Hites, Jeanne M. and Fisher, Walter W. "Modifying Course Materials for International Students". *Performance and Instruction* 23 (December, 1984): 7-9.

The article discusses the methods for modifying existing training courses for international students, such as conducting audience and needs analysis, matching audience needs to existing course objectives, and material modification. Specific modifications helpful in redesigning course materials are also detailed.

Hoffman, Irene and Popa, Opritsa. "Library Orientation and Instruction for International Students: The University of California-Davis Experience". *RQ* 25 (Spring, 1986): 356-360.

To help foreign students adjust to academic environment, the University of California-Davis Library developed a personalized instructional program with a dual emphasis: teaching international students how to find and use library information; educating library staff to recognize and understand the special needs of these patrons.

Johnson, G. L. "The Relevance of United States Graduate Curricula in Agricultural Economics". *American Journal of Agricultural Economics* 65, No. 5 (1984): 1142-1148.

This article presents a critical analysis of the U.S. graduate programs in agricultural economics for the training of foreign students. The weaknesses identified by the author include the inadequate requirements for macroeconomics, trade theory, and general economics, the overemphasis on modern methods, and the failure to address Marxist ideas. The article concludes with some recommendations to improve the curricula for students from less developed countries enrolled in U.S. graduate institutions.

King, Kenneth. "Overseas Training for Development: An Analysis of Britain's Technical Cooperation Training Programme from the National and the Donor Perspective". In *Readings in Overseas Student Policy*, eds. G. Williams, M. Kenyon, and L. Williams (London: Overseas Student Trust, 1987): 47-70.

The Technical Cooperation Training Program (TCTP) is by far the largest British government award scheme, bringing over 10,000 students and trainees from developing countries to the U.K. each year. The article examines the TCTP within the local and external context of donor-aided overseas training and concludes that Britain's training strategy could be usefully improved in a number of ways. Primarily, the author argues that training should cease to be heavily project-related. It should extend beyond the project to include the wider infrastructure, such as the sector in which the project is located and the decision-making apparatus of government. This implies the need for a much longer training cycle, conceived as a form of investment protection, which in turn leads to the conclusion that if real technological and administrative capacity is to be created in developing countries, increased funding is essential.

Klein, H. and Zuckert, U. "The Co-operation Schemes Linking Berlin Humboldt University (GDR) with Universities and Academic Establishments in Developing Countries". *Higher Education in Europe* 11, No. 3 (1986): 16-18.

With the increase in both scope and in importance of co-operation in science and education, principles underlying the co-operation between higher education institutions should be carefully analyzed. Although most of the co-operation in effect is beneficial, some of it has contributed to the brain drain of qualified scholars from the Third World. This article focuses on one specific case -- Berlin Humboldt University -- where the co-operation with developing-countries institutions has been positive to graduates whose potentials are crucial for the resolution of many national problems.

Kline, Laura S. and Rod, Katherine M. "Library Orientation Programs for Foreign Students: A Survey". *RQ* 24 (Winter, 1984): 210-216.

The article reports the results of a survey involving 54 U.S. colleges and universities that while 98% of international education offices offered orientation programs for newly enrolled foreign students, only 56% of libraries provided special instruction for this group. On such a basis, the article discusses the need for programs and makes suggestions for establishing them. A questionnaire is appended.

Koch, S. "The Use of Activation Methods in a Classroom Educational Process in Foreign Students". *Ceskoslovenska Psychologie* 30, No. 2 (1985): 125-177.

Lansdale, David. "Institutional Culture and Third World Student Needs at American Universities". In *Bridges to Knowledge: Foreign Students in Comparative Perspective*, eds. E. Barber, P. Altbach, and R. Myers (Chicago, IL: University of Chicago Press, 1984): 196-206.

Compares the instructional capacities and objectives of the university -- the "institutional culture" and Third World students' expectations in the school of engineering of a large, private research university in the U.S. Finds that a definite mismatch between the needs of Third World students and the institutional culture is embodied in departmental programs, even though considerable variation exists across the members of the faculty. Attributes this discrepancy to a combination of the structural composition of the department admissions process and market forces.

Lee, Motoko Y. and Ray, Melvin C. "Relevancy of U.S. Degree Programs and Curriculum Needs: Perceptions of Students from Developing Countries". *Journal of the Association of International Education and Administrators* 7 (Spring, 1987): 1-8.

The article presents some of the data obtained in the NAFSA/USAID survey to assess the needs of students from developing countries. A probability sample of 1,897 students from 30 schools across the nation participated by completing a mailing questionnaire in 1979. The students represent 102 developing countries. The data examined include relevancy needs, curriculum needs, and personal characteristics. Students considered their degree programs relevant to: (1) jobs at home countries; (2) present needs of home countries; and (3) future needs of home countries. Five recommendations are made concerning how to enhance the relevancy of degree programs to students from the Third World by taking their perspectives into serious consideration.

Minor, David. "Reflections on Education in Britain by an Exchange Student". *College Board Review* No. 136 (Summer, 1985): 22-25, 33.

British education seems to be quite narrow and specialized, contrasted with U.S. education. The English system is based largely on testing and more fully reflects its social structure (more class oriented and less flexible than in the U.S.).

Owen, W. F. "Expanding Opportunities for Higher Education Abroad for Students from Developing Countries: A Case Study: The

CONACYT-El Approach". *Inter-American Economic Affairs* 38 (Summer, 1984): 23-43.

Examines a particular approach to expanding access to universities in which English is the language of instruction. (The approach was followed in a cooperative effort between the National Council for Science and Technology in Mexico and the Economics Institute in Colorado during the years 1978 through 1982.) Finds that the CONACYT group has raised its average preparation of their study programs; that it proved itself to be remarkably competitive in grade performances; that its success record for admissions was quite impressive; that its performance in their graduate degree programs was successful; and that its cost was reasonable and its benefits were desirable.

Reed, Linda A. "Internationally Experienced Students -- A Valuable Resource". *Intercom* No. 106 (March, 1985): 3-5.

The author discusses how teachers can use foreign students enrolled in U.S. schools as educational resources to enhance the international awareness and understanding of U.S. students. She also examines the changes that need to be made so that foreign students can be better utilized as educational resources in American schools.

Romana, Elpidio. "Evaluation and Prospects of the Mombusho Scholarship Program in the Philippines". *Research in Higher Education (Daigaku Ronshu)* No. 15 (1986): 55-72.

The Mombusho Scholarship Program, having started in 1954, is the oldest and largest Japanese scholarship program in the Philippines, with more than 500 recipients by late 1985. The article assesses this scholarship program by examining the accomplishments of the former and current Filipino grantees, and their feelings about the Japanese education and Japanese degree. It also makes some suggestions as to how the program can be expanded more rationally from a Filipino's perspective.

Tsukahara, S., Muta, H., and Yamada, T. "Reception of Foreign Students into Graduate Programs in Japan". *Research in Higher Education (Daigaku Ronshu)* 14 (1985): 209-229. (In Japanese)

Examines the circumstances under which Japanese universities receive foreign students into their doctoral programs. Explores problems for Japanese universities to tackle. Finds that: (a) the popular image that Japanese universities only provide a limited number of places for overseas students has proved to be misleading in some fields; (b) the language barrier most frequently causes foreign students difficulties in class, while low cognitive achievement in basic subjects is also a deterrent in science and technology; (c) a doctorate in science and technology is not particularly difficult for an overseas student to obtain; (d) the feeling of professors who have a considerable number of overseas students in their doctoral courses is that their presence has been a burden to them; and (e) Japanese universities as a whole are quite willing to receive more foreign students into their programs. Puts forward some suggestions on policies concerning foreign students.

23. Language-Related Issues

Books

Chaudron, Craig. *Second Language Classrooms, Research on Teaching and Learning*. Cambridge, England: Cambridge University Press, 1987.

Jenkins, Hugh M. *English Language Training and Sponsored Students from the Developing World: A Report of a Seminar*. Washington, D.C.: National Association for Foreign Student Affairs, 1984. 16 p.

A report of a seminar on English language training for foreign students, this document covers a number of key points relating to

English language. The TOEFL test and its uses are discussed, as are issues of second language acquisition and placement questions in language programs. This report makes it clear that the issues involved with English language training for foreign students are complex and deserve further analysis.

National Association for Foreign Student Affairs. *Education for International Development: English Language Training and Sponsored Students from the Developing World.* Washington, D.C.: National Association for Foreign Student Affairs, 1984.

A report of a seminar on English language training and sponsored students from the developing world, this volume examines the existing resources in the fields, the ways to improve the assessment of the need for English language training, and the most effective and least expensive ways of meeting these needs, either in the U.S. or in the students' home countries, or in both. It discusses the process of second language acquisition, identification of students variables affecting proper placement and program goals, key elements of various language training programs, and concerns of TESOL teachers. It also compares U.S.-based second language programs with overseas training programs and reviews evaluation procedures and tests.

Robertson, Daniel L. *English Language Use, Needs, and Proficiency Among Foreign Students at the University of Illinois at Urbana-Champaign.* Unpublished Ph.D. Dissertation, University of Illinois at Urbana-Champaign, 1983. 133 p. Order No. DA8410033

This research reveals the extent to which foreign students' reported use of English, their perceptions of the importance of English, and their proficiency in English are related to their membership in groups based on academic discipline, academic level, and teaching assistantship (TA) status.

Discipline was found to be significantly related to nine of the variables, level was found to be related to five, and TA status, five.

Differences in use of speaking and writing skills were observed across disciplines. Differences in use of speaking and listening skills were observed across levels. Differences in use of speaking skills were observed across TA status.

Differences in perceived importance of English language skills in general and of writing skills were observed across disciplines. No differences in importance were observed across levels or TA status.

Differences in perceived ability in listening and reading skills were observed across disciplines. Differences in reading skills were observed across levels. Differences in ability in speaking and listening skills were observed across TA status. TOEFL scores were also found to be higher among TAs.

Wilson, Kenneth M. *A Comparative Analysis of TOEFL Examinee Characteristics 1977-79*. Princeton, NJ: Educational Testing Service, 1982.

Wilson, Kenneth M. *GMAT and GRE Aptitude Test Performance in Relation to Primary Language and Scores on TOEFL*. Princeton, NJ: Educational Testing Service, 1982.

Articles

Choy, Siew Chee and Davenport, Betty M. "The TOEFL: Incomplete Test of English Proficiency". *College Teaching* 32 (Summer, 1986): 108-110.

The ability to think in a foreign language is reflected more accurately in the ability to speak and write the language. Thus, the article suggests that colleges and universities need to supplement the TOEFL with tests of English conversation, specialized vocabulary, and written composition.

Elson, Nicholas. "Reading and Meaning for University Level ESL Students". *TESL Talk* 15 (Summer, 1984): 26-34.

Gass, Susan M. and Varonis, E. M. "Variation in Native Speaker Speech Modification to Non-Native Speakers". *Studies in Second Language Acquisition* 7, No. 1 (1985): 37-57.

Hargett, Gary R. and Alswang, Steven G. "An Institutional Approach to Improving the English Proficiency of Foreign Students: The Modified Transition Model". *American Language Journal* 2, No. 1 (1984): 67-83.

This article analyzes several issues that institutions face regarding foreign students' language requirements, such as understanding the relationship between English proficiency and successful academic outcomes, identifying English proficiency skills necessary for academic success, considering whether the critical proficiency levels may vary across disciplines, deciding what is acceptable evidence of adequate English proficiency, and ascertaining institutional responsibilities to foreign students who may have less than full English proficiency. It also describes a plan for offering foreign students the ESL assistance deemed necessary for their academic success and highlights the features of the plan -- integrating the ESL assistance into the regular academic program and facilitating the mainstreaming process for new foreign students.

Huckin, Thomas N. and Olsen, Leslie A. "The Need for Professionally Oriented ESL Instruction in the United States". *TESOL Quarterly* 18 (June, 1984): 273-294.

Kaplan, Robert B. "English As a Second Language: A Guide to Sources". In *Bridges to Knowledge: Foreign Students in Comparative Perspective*, eds. E. Barber, P. Altbach, and R. Myers (Chicago: University of Chicago Press, 1984): 247-258.

This chapter features an introduction to the field of English as a second language and a guide to major resources in the field. A select but informative bibliography is also included. The author links ESL to language teaching and to linguistic theory and development.

Oster, Judith. "The ESL Composition Course and the Idea of a University". *College English* 47 (January, 1985): 66-76.

Robertson, D. L. "English Language Use, Needs and Proficiency Among Foreign Students at the University of Illinois at Urbana-Champaign". *TESOL Quarterly* 18, No. 1 (1984): 144-145.

24. International Educational Exchange and Study Abroad

Books

Abe, Hiroshi, ed. *Nittyukyoiku Bunkakouryu to Masatsu (Japan-China Educational Exchange and Its Conflicts)*. Tokyo: Daiichishobo, 1983. 411 p.

Academic Mobility in Europe: Report of the Conference. Strasbourg, France: Division for Higher Education and Research, Council of Europe, 1983.

Baron, B. and Smith, A. *Higher Education in the European Community: Study Abroad in the European Community*. Luxembourg: Office for Official Publications of the European Communities, 1987.

This volume focuses on the various study abroad programs in the European Community. The chapters provide detailed analysis and data concerning a range of issues and reflect the major concern in Europe for study abroad. Among the topics considered are students (including mobility, demographic factors, and financing of studies), foreign language and study abroad programs, career implications of study abroad programs, costs and financing, and academic recognition and transferability of degrees. This volume is probably the most up-to-date and complete consideration of the European situation.

Commonwealth Secretariat. *Commonwealth Student Mobility: Commitment and Resources.* London: Commonwealth Secretariat, 1986.

> The report of the 5th conference on the Commonwealth Standing Committee on student mobility provides some useful statistical information concerning trends in student mobility in Commonwealth countries. It also makes a series of recommendations concerning maintaining flows of students. It points out that as fees for overseas study have increased in several Commonwealth nations, notably Britain, the numbers of Commonwealth students in those countries has declined. Recommendations concerning women students, the development of a special Commonwealth fund for student mobility, and related topics are also made in the report. Short summaries of current policies concerning overseas study in Britain, Canada, and Australia are included.

Commonwealth Secretariat. *Commonwealth Student Mobility in the Nineteen-Eighties.* London: Commonwealth Standing Committee on Student Mobility, Commonwealth Secretariat, 1984.

Elmary, Andree. *Les Exchanges Scholaires: leur role dans l'education.* Paris: Federation Internationale de Organization de Correspondences et d'echanges scholaires (UNESCO), 1981.

> This study deals essentially with the type of exchanges provided by the FIOCES since its creation in 1929. Those types include exchanges of letters and written or oral documents and exchanges of people, students, teachers in training or practice at the elementary, secondary, and occasionally university level.

> The study focuses also on trips abroad. Although such trips are not considered as scholarly exchange, they contribute to the goals of the FIOCES -- to facilitate a better understanding of languages, foreign civilizations, and national and international problems, and a better relationship between people of different nations.

Giles, G. *Australia's Overseas Student Program. Aid, Not Trade.* Newcastle, Australia: University of New South Wales, 1985.

National Association for Foreign Student Affairs. *Regulatory Roadblocks to International Exchange: Report and Recommendations by the National Association for Foreign Student Affairs.* Washington, D.C.: National Association for Foreign Student Affairs, 1985.

Richmond, Yale. *U.S.-Soviet Cultural Exchanges, 1958-1986: Who Wins?* Boulder, CO: Westview, 1987. 170 p.

A broad consideration of issues relating to Soviet-American contacts of all kinds, this volume has relevance to foreign students and international study. It discusses the various Soviet-American cultural agreements, the motivations of both sides, and the historical development of cultural arrangements. One chapter dealing specifically with scholars and students discusses the various specific programs for the exchange of students and scholars, problems encountered in these efforts, and related matters.

Shotnes, Stephen, ed. *Overseas Students -- Who Learns What?* London: United Kingdom Council on Overseas Student Affairs, 1985.

This volume contains some of the papers from the 1984 conference of the UK Council on Overseas Student Affairs. Among the topics considered are the benefits to institutions of overseas students, the relevance of overseas study, learning to live in a global society, and setting an agenda for the future of international exchanges. Several of the papers point out that overseas students can provide a "window" for people in the host society to learn about their own country and its problems.

Study Abroad in the European Community. Brussels: European Institute of Education and Social Policy, 1985.

Swinger, Alice K. *Planning for Study Abroad.* Bloomington, IN: Phi Delta Kappa Educational Foundation, 1985. 38 p.

Written for first-time or relatively inexperienced travelers, this booklet discusses the benefits of study abroad, goal setting, program selection, background gaining, communication with hosting institution/individual, financial problems, arrangement of official documents, things to take, the coping with daily life, and preparations for reentry.

Thomas A., ed. *Interkultureller Austausch als Interkulturelles Handeln. Theoretische Grundlagen der Austauschforschung (SSIP Bulletin No. 56) (Intercultural Exchange as Intercultural Trade: Theoretical Underpinnings of Exchange Research).* Saarbrücken: Verlag Breitenbach, 1985.

Thomas A., ed. *Interkultureller Personenaustausch in Forschung und Praxis (SSIP Bulletin No. 54) (Intercultural Exchange in Research and Practice.* Saarbrücken: Verlag Breitenbach, 1984.

Zikopoulos, Marianthi and Barber, Elinor G. *The ITT International Fellowship Program: An Assessment After Ten Years (IIE Research Report No. 4).* New York: Institute of International Education, 1984.

Between 1973 and 1982, 498 students received fellowships from the ITT Corporation. Two-hundred and forty-four of the students were Americans who went overseas for a year of study. Two-hundred and fifty-four were foreigners who came to the U.S. to pursue a masters degree. This 53-page report is an evaluation of the program. Among the general findings are:

• The ITT fellows are successful in their occupations and hold positions in their societies of high prestige and income. They believe that participation in the ITT fellowship program contributed to their success.

• The fellows became familiar with their host societies.

• The fellows became proficient in a foreign language.

• The fellows are concerned about international relations, and they have played leadership roles in their societies in seeking solutions to international problems and issues.

• The gains made in international knowledge are sustained over the long run.

Articles

Adams, R. "Formal Agreements with the U.S.S.R. for Scholarly Access Are Necessary Even When the Results Are Not Ideal". *Smithsonian* 16 (February, 1986): 10.

Allaway, W. H. "The International Committee for the Study of Educational Exchange: A Search for Policy Guidance". *Higher Education in Europe* 11, No. 1 (1986): 51-61.

This article reviews the creation and implementation of the International Committee for the Study of Educational Exchange (ICSEE). The focus is on the circumstances surrounding its creation as well as on the research supporting its relevancy. From the early 1960s to the 1980s, the ICSEE has developed new policies aimed at providing funds for foreign students and study abroad, maintaining an institutional policy for the release and replacement of faculty members for the purpose of teaching, and doing research abroad.

Ammerman, W. "The Fulbright Program: A Quiet and Efficient Success". *Phi Delta Kappan* 65 (February, 1984): 421-422.

Burn, Barbara. "Research in Progress: Does Study Abroad Make a Difference"? *Change* 17 (March/April, 1985): 48-49.

The Study Abroad Evaluation Project is designed to examine international study and student exchange programs within Europe and between Europe and the United States to identify the most effective program characteristics. Focus is on institutional impact, student attitudes, academic performance, and employment goals and opportunities.

Cassell, William C. and Cassell, Jeanne T. "A Small College Opens a Window on the World". *Educational Record* 68 (Spring, 1987): 12-16.

Dubil, A., et al. "A School/University Teacher Exchange Revitalizes Both Participants". *Phi Delta Kappan* 66 (May, 1985): 650-651.

Eliutin, V. P. "The International Activity of Soviet Higher Education". *Soviet Education* 27, No. 9-10 (1985): 121-158.

Describes the international activity of Soviet higher education, including cooperation in the training of specialists; exchange of experience in teaching and research; participation in the activities of international organizations dealing with culture, science, and education; development of creative contacts between educators, scientists, and scholars in higher education in different countries; and international communication among youth students. Points out that these activities help to improve higher education in the USSR and to further the intellectual and socioeconomic progress of mankind. Concludes that international ties in education throughout the modern world are growing in importance and have great prospects for development, and that in our day the constructive possibilities of international cooperation in education for the good of all mankind have expanded considerably.

Embrey, L. "Physical Education, Sport and Foreign Aid (Australian Foreign Student Exchange)." *ACHPER National Journal* No. 107 (March, 1985): 14-16, 45-47.

Escolano, A. "International Student Mobility: Problems and Perspectives". *Higher Education in Europe* 11, No. 2 (1986): 33-38.

Analyzes the main reasons for the international mobility of European students in higher education, pointing out that it is not only due to geographic proximity, but more closely linked to questions of an economic and, more generally, cultural nature. Identifies various types of obstacles that make the flexible intercommunication of university students difficult, including rigorous admissions procedures and enrollment surcharge. Argues that the critical points that most affect student mobility are curricular diversification and the kind of academic degrees and diplomas to which it leads. Puts forward several suggestions that may alleviate these difficulties.

Fan, Jian Ming. "The Role of International Exchange in Speeding Up the Education of Trained Workers". *Research in Higher Education (Daigaku Ronshu)* No. 15 (1986): 89-93.

"German Academic Exchange Service: German Students Like Going Abroad". *Bildung und Wissenschaft* No. 5 (1986): 13.

Harrison, C. "U.S.-Brazil Partners in Education". *Change* 18 (July/August, 1986): 54-55.

Heller, Barbara R. and Geringer, Wendy. "Selected Problems of International Cooperative Education: The U.S.A. As Sender and Receiver of Study-Abroad Students". *Journal of Cooperative Education* 20 (Spring, 1984): 41-52.

The difficulties of American students overseas and of foreign students in the United States are illustrated. The implementation of one international cooperative program between the U.S. and a developing country and some of the ingredients of a successful cooperative arrangement are also demonstrated.

Knochenmus, J. P. "University Studies Abroad -- Their Contribution to International Understanding and Cooperation". *Higher Education in Europe* 11, No. 1 (1986): 62-67.

This article reports on the debates of the 1985 round table on the topic "University Studies Abroad: Their Contribution to International Understanding and Co-operation". The debates focus on the reasons young people decide to pursue higher education studies abroad, in an attempt to identify the favoring and the discouraging factors. Other topics of the debate include the measures taken by the host country to facilitate the accomplishment of research; recognition of studies pursued and diplomas obtained abroad, as well as the role of higher education in the promotion of international understanding and co-operation.

Lobkowicz, Nikolaus. "La responsabilité educative de l'université vis-à-vis des étudiants étrangers". *CRE-Information* 57 (1982): 27-43.

A plea for European universities to understand their responsibility toward students from the Third World and to pay attention to providing foreign students with a profitable educational experience. The issue of relating Third World cultures to European cultures is discussed, and careful planning is sought to reduce the alienation among foreign students in Europe and to ensure that European university education is relevant to the needs of the Third World.

Massue, J. P. "Mobility in the Framework of Transfrontier Regional Cooperation". *Universitas. Studie documentazione di vitauniversitaria* 5 (October-December, 1984): 81-87.

Opper, S. "International Mobility and Recognition of Studies, Diplomas and Degrees". *Higher Education in Europe* 11, No. 2 (1986): 69-74.

Analyzes the results of a survey of aims, development organizations, participants, major problems, successes, and impacts of study abroad programs conducted by the European Institute of Education and Social Policy. The major findings of the survey include:

1. The primary value of study abroad lies in the opportunity provided for total immersion in other cultures than one's own. This not only increases awareness of "others", but also forces one into a comparative experience. "Improvement of students' career prospects" is one of very important objectives for studying abroad.

2. Students and directors expect organized programs to provide appropriate recognition for work carried out abroad.

3. Study abroad does involve costs over and above those normally incurred by a stay solely at the home institution.

4. The major features that distinguish students who participate in a study abroad program from those who do not are openness toward foreign countries and international affairs and sufficient competence in foreign languages.

Paige, Michael R. and La Berge, Bernard. "Analyzing Unethical Practices in International Educational Exchange". *NAFSA Newsletter* 38 (November, 1986): 15-19.

Of immediate concern to practitioners in international educational exchange are special fees for international students, foreign teaching assistants, and private counseling. Problems in these areas must be considered within a complex legal and ethical framework. Institutions should consider alternative sources of support for foreign students or consider not recruiting or enrolling such students. Employment of foreign TAs has a direct impact on higher education. Screening TAs for language and teaching potential is a must. Many institutions have developed strict rules and guidelines for private consulting. Clear, strict policies that recognize the interests of the individual and the institution are needed so that individuals can legitimately offer their specialized skills in both an institutional and private capacity.

Peng, Wen Sheng. "Evaluating Study Abroad in Japan". *Research in Higher Education (Daigaku Ronshu)* No. 15 (1986): 73-77.

Roeloffs, K. "Deutscher Akademischer Austauschdienst (DAAD): German Academic Exchange Service: Profile and Programmes". *Higher Education in Europe* 11, No. 1 (1986): 43-50.

This article takes a look at the structure and programs of the German Academic Exchange Service (DAAD). The purpose of the DAAD is to foster academic relations with foreign countries' institutions. It provides an opportunity for student mobility for foreign students as well as German students going abroad, and staff mobility through direct sponsorship.

Salam, A. "Inter-University Co-operation: The Europe-Developing Countries Experience -- Balance Sheet and Perspectives". *Higher Education in Europe* 11, No. 3 (1986): 7-12.

While there is a relative decrease in foreign student enrollment in Italian higher education institutions, the scheme of associateships offered in some institutions such as Trieste Centre provides a unique opportunity for foreign scholars to periodically visit the center and refresh themselves with new ideas and interactions. In addition to the associateship scheme, the Trieste Centre maintains relationship with other research institutions around the world. The author concludes with some recommendations to expand the Trieste experience -- which is in the field of physics -- to other fields.

Savov, M. and Nikolov, I. "Participation of Bulgarian Higher Education in International Co-operation Within the European Region". *Higher Education in Europe* 11, No. 1 (1986): 11-20.

This article focuses on the co-operation of Bulgarian higher education with other European higher education systems. It puts a particular emphasis on the training of foreign students in higher education institutions in Bulgaria, as well as on Bulgarian students studying abroad and exchanges and research staff. Co-operation with international governmental and non-governmental organization is also examined.

Shayo, L. K. "The Transfer of Science and Technology Between Developed and Developing Countries through Co-operation of Institutions of Higher Learning". *Higher Education in Europe* 11, No. 3 (1986): 19-23.

This article focuses on the five methods of science and technology transfer to developing countries. They are voluntary expatriates from developed to developing countries; personnel assistance; training of staff from developing countries in developed countries; importation of technology; and, finally, cooperation between institutions of higher educations. The article also provides an example of inter-university links that has adopted the above methods of science and technology transfer.

Walsh, J. "U.S.-China Exchanges Accentuate Sciences". *Science* 232 (June 27, 1986): 1597.

25. Disciplinary Studies

Books

Bowling, Weldon James. *The Utilization of U.S. Higher Education and Training by Foreign Naval Officers.* Ed.D. Dissertation, North Texas State University, 1984.

Mai, M. *Ingenieurstudium im Ausland (Engineering Studies in Foreign Countries).* Düsseldorf: VDI-Verlag, 1985.

Rochester, Maxine K. *Foreign Students in American Library Education: Impact on Home Countries.* Westport, CT: Greenwood Press, 1986.

Articles

Barber, Elinor G. and Morgan, Robert P. "The Impact of Foreign Graduate Students on Engineering Education in the United States". *Science* 236 (April 3, 1987): 33-37.

Surveys of chairs and faculty members of engineering departments of U.S. universities were conducted in the fall of 1985 to examine the relation between the high proportion of foreign graduate students and the operation and quality of engineering education in the U.S. Information was obtained on admissions criteria and policies, financial aid, and the performance of U.S. and foreign students as teaching and research assistants. Overall, the survey respondents believed that foreign students are an asset, and that without them training and research would suffer. Language and communications were the problems most frequently mentioned as adversely affecting the performance of foreign students.

Barber, Elinor G. and Morgan, Robert P. "Viewpoint: Engineering Education and the International Student: Policy Issues". *Engineering Education* 74 (April, 1984): 655-659.

The article discusses the relevance of United States engineering education to foreign students, the impact of foreign students on engineering education, military and economic security concerns, and immigration and brain-drain questions. It concludes that more research is needed to understand the contribution of foreign students and to provide for informed policies and decisions.

Brandas, Antonio S. "The U.S. Graduate Training in Agricultural Economics: The Perspective of a Former Foreign Student". *American Journal of Agricultural Economics* 65 (December, 1983): 1149-1152.

Cunningham, Daisy L. and Burge, Penny L. "International Home Economics Students Critique U.S. Collegiate Programs". *Journal of Studies in Technical Careers* 6 (Summer, 1984): 170-176.

The article reports a survey of graduated international students about their perceptions of the usefulness of their educations. Textbooks and teaching materials drew the most favorable responses, while somewhat lower ratings were given for advisers and counselors. The concluding section suggests some improvement strategies.

Hartman, Mary E.; Sutnick, Alton I., et al. "Comparison of Performances of Transfer Students and First Year Acceptees". *Journal of Medical Education* 61 (March, 1986): 151-156.

Henderson, Metta L. and Ohvall, R. A. "Foreign Pharmacy Graduate and Post-Baccalaureate Doctor of Pharmacy Students Within United States Colleges of Pharmacy". *American Journal of Pharmaceutical Education* 48 (Summer, 1984): 130-133.

A survey of Ph.D., M.S., and post-baccalaureate pharmacy doctoral students in schools of pharmacy was conducted, and the American and foreign students were compared. A much higher percentage of foreign students selected academia as a career aspiration than did Americans.

"International Education in Psychology". *American Psychologist* 39 (September, 1984): 996-1042.

Kolata, G. "Americans Scarce in Math Grad Schools". *Science* 230 (November 15, 1985): 787.

Kouzekanani, Kamiar and Miller, Larry. "International Extension Education: Policies and Graduate Study". *Journal of the American Association of Teacher Educators in Agriculture* 26 (Spring, 1985): 23-29.

The study was designed to describe extension education as perceived by educators and international students of extension and to determine the topics that should be provided in a graduate program. One hundred and one extension educators were surveyed concerning course topics and the educational needs of rural people.

Mahan, James M. and Stachowski, Laura. "Overseas Student Teaching: A Model, Important Outcomes, Recommendations". *International Education* 15 (Fall, 1985): 9-30.

Presents a model of overseas teaching by which student teachers are placed in foreign schools for eight-week teaching assignments. Finds that student teachers are able to successfully complete assignments in overseas schools, develop a knowledge and appreciation of different cultures, add to their repertoire new teaching skills and techniques, increase their confidence as effective educators, and generally enhance their personal and professional growth and development. Recommends that greater exposure to international issues should be encouraged in teacher-training institutions.

Mahan, J. M. and Stachowski, L. L. "Feedback from British and Irish Educators for Improving Overseas Teaching Experiences". *Journal of Education for Teaching* 13, No. 1 (1987): 29-48.

McDermott, M. and Thomas, E. "Foreign Physics Graduate Students in the United States". *Physics Today* 39 (June, 1986): 48-55.

Discusses various aspects of the increasing proportion of foreign citizens among physics graduate students in the U.S. The percentage for first-year graduate students in 1986 was 42%, up from 17% in 1971. Reviews the history of the flow of foreign students into U.S. graduate programs in physics, the selection of students, teaching assistantships as a chief source of support for most of the physics graduate students, the impact on standards and programs, attitudes of foreign governments, U.S. federal and state attitudes, and the impact on employment. Suggests that foreign Ph.D.s and U.S. Ph.D.s together will be insufficient to meet future manpower needs and that U.S. may have a very strong interest in welcoming foreign graduate students in physics. Argues that physicists should concern rather with the very small number of U.S. doctoral students in physics programs.

Miller, D. F. "International Students: Their Effect on College Health Education". *Health Education* 18 (April-May, 1987): 26-28.

Senninger, Charles and Nataf, Raphael. "Literature francaise a l'usage des étudiants étrangers (French Literature for Foreign Students)". *Francais dans le monde* No. 182 (January, 1984): 59-64.

It is suggested that it has become increasingly more important to expose foreign students of French to the full expanse of French literary history, both for its richness and for its actual value. Two teachers of French literature for foreign students discuss the rationale and elements of successful literature instruction.

Sweet, W. "Larger Share of Ph.D.s Goes to Foreigners". *Physics Today* 37 (December, 1984): 64.

26. Specific National Studies

Books

Akitikpo, David Ukebulunwo. *Career Considerations in the Choice of Academic Training Among Nigerian Students in the NAFSA Region Three.* Ed.D. Dissertation, University of Arkansas, 1985. 108 p. Order No. DA8618000

The purpose of this study was to investigate and analyze the motivations behind career choices of Nigerian students in American colleges and universities. The population of this study was Nigerian students in Region Three of the National Association for Foreign Student Affairs.

Findings indicated that the Nigerian students' career choices seem to follow no set patterns: career choice for formal study was not made with their career aptitudes as primary information, and Nigerian students place importance on different values from American students.

This study has implications for secondary and post-secondary schools in Nigeria, as well as colleges and universities in the United States. It also has implications for the Ministry of Education and curriculum planners in Nigeria.

Al-Ghamdi, Hamdan A. *Study of Selected Aspects of the Academic Pursuits of Saudi Arabian Government Master's Degree Scholarship Students in the United States of America.* Ed.D. Dissertation, University of Houston, 1985. 251 p. Order No. DA8517693

This research investigated factors that may contribute to Saudi Arabian scholarship students changing their majors after they have begun their graduate programs. The study was limited to master's-level students only. The study is intended to provide the Saudi Arabian Educational Mission to the United States (SAEM) and the Saudi government's sponsoring agencies with information to facilitate the successful administration of the Saudi government's scholarship program in the United States.

Generally the data indicated that the SAEM and the sponsoring agencies agree on most issues regarding students' changing their majors. The exceptions to the above included the following: (1) The SAEM and the sponsoring agencies had differences regarding what constitutes a change of major. (2) The SAEM personnel felt that their recommendations to the sponsoring agencies regarding students' changing their majors were not properly considered. (3) The sponsoring agency personnel felt that the standards used to select scholarship students were high. The SAEM personnel thought they were low. (4) Only two demographic characteristics were found to be related. These included the cumulative grade point average, which was found to be slightly higher for those students who changed their majors, and the compatibility of the undergraduate major to the graduate major.

Based on the findings of this study, the following recommendations were provided: (1) The sponsoring agencies should put more emphasis on program content than on the title of the program when assigning majors. (2) More authority should be given to the Saudi Mission to approve students' change of majors. (3) The sponsoring agencies should review standards and qualifications used in student selection. (4) The sponsoring agencies should implement a more comprehensive orientation program to include more areas related to student problems. (5) The SAEM should review and/or revise its office procedures and policies to better serve the needs of the students. (6) The sponsoring agencies should establish uniform policies regarding sponsored students to the extent possible. (7) Further study should be conducted utilizing currently enrolled students, to be replicated in other countries where Saudi students are studying. (8) Further study should be conducted using bachelor's and doctoral scholarship students changing their majors.

Bilibin, Dmitri. *Foreign Students in the USSR.* Moscow: Novosti Press Agency, 1984.

Boyd, Alan W. and Noss, Elaine M., eds. *Malaysian Students in U.S. Colleges and Universities.* Washington, D.C.: National Association for Foreign Student Affairs, 1986. 59 p.

With 23,000 Malaysian students enrolled in American colleges and universities, this book has special relevance. It provides a thumbnail sketch of the history and current status of the Malaysian educational system, a discussion of Malaysian government policy relating to overseas study, the organization of Malaysia's foreign student services, and some guidelines for relating to Malaysian students in the United States. The book is aimed at professionals working with Malaysian students, and is a very useful guide as well as a source of factual information.

Chinapah, Vinayagum. *Foreign Students at Institutions of Higher Learning in Sweden.* Paris: Organization for Economic Cooperation and Development, 1986.

The publication describes the learning and living conditions of foreign students, especially visiting students, in Sweden, and presents some of the innovative programs, practices, and arrangements established for them during the early period of study in the country. The paper also examines the following six problem areas of visiting students: language barriers; inadequate academic background for university study; procedures for renewing study residence permit; economic constraints; information gaps; and social and cultural isolation/adaptation. The paper ends with some recommendations to policymakers and implementation agents about possible intervention strategies for meeting the academic and non-academic needs of foreign students in Sweden.

Goodman, N. *The Institutionalization of Foreign Education and the Effects of the Charter: A Study of Malaysian Student Attitudes and Adjustment to Overseas Educational Opportunity.* Unpublished Ph.D. Dissertation, Stanford University, 1984.

Kotenkar, Arun. *Auslandische Studenten in der Bundesrepublik (Univeritat Frankfurt) (Foreign Students in the FRG (University of Frankfurt))*. Stuttgart: Alektor-Verlag, 1980. 148 p.

This study on foreign-student problems and concerns is based on 187 questionnaires distributed to foreign students at the University of Frankfurt (60% from developing countries) in 1977/78, as well as interviews with employees in the university's foreign student office. The students were asked about their level of satisfaction with the work of the foreign student office, the preparatory school, and visa authorities, as well as their financial and living situations, social contacts, reasons for studying abroad, acts of discrimination against them, adjustment difficulties, and the willingness to return to their countries. In a section on the identity of both student and foreigner, the author maintains that it is especially difficult for students from the developing world to establish relationships with Germans.

LeBlanc, Darrell and Cap, Orest. *Faculty Perceptions of Nigerians Enrolled in Technical Teacher Training Programs, Report II.* Winnipeg: University of Manitoba, 1986. 126 p.

The Nigerian Teacher Training Project was to provide for a Bachelor of Education degree program in the short run, but to develop a pool of trained technical instructors in the long run. An evaluation of the program was made by gathering the perceptions of the implementation of the program by faculty and advisers. A sample of ten professors/advisers answered a questionnaire with a Likert-type scale regarding their perceptions of the Nigerian students' experiences in the program. Results of data analysis showed that the respondents' attitudes were primarily positive. Based on these results, recommendations were made for improvement in the following areas: (1) selection of candidates; (2) formation of a planning and review conference; (3) the government of Nigeria's involvement in the total program; (4) preparation for departure from Nigeria; (5) responsibilities of the educational institution and opportunities within the institute of enrollment and community; (6) project personnel; and (7) living conditions and cultural integration.

Moghtassed, Shokoufeh. *A Study of Characteristics of Iranian College Students and Their Intentions to Stay in the United States.* Ph.D. Dissertation, George Peabody College, 1986.

Ogita, Sekiko. *Bunka Sakoku Nippon no Ryugakusei (Foreign Students in Culturally Closed Country Japan).* Tokyo: Gakuyoshobo, 1986. 206 p.

Overseas Students: Destination U.K.: Report of the 1985 UKCOSA Annual Conference. London: United Kingdom Council on Overseas Student Affairs, 1985.

A summary of the panels at the 1985 annual conference of U.K. Council on Overseas Student Affairs. Among the topics considered are exchange flows in Europe and the Commonwealth countries, transatlantic student exchanges, refugee policy, the role of the overseas student adviser, language testing and placement, overseas students in the community, the role of the U.K. in student exchanges, and others. Summaries of sessions, but not the complete papers, are given.

Radford, Mark, et al. *Overseas Students in South Australia.* Adelaide, Australia: Flinders University International Students' Association, 1984.

Tanuvasa, Alofa S. *Western Samoan Students at BYU-Hawaii: Academic Achievement and Aspirations for Teaching in Western Samoa.* Unpublished Ed.D. Dissertation, Brigham Young University, 1984. 163 p. Order No. DA8427799

The purpose of this study was to determine the degree of success of the academic experience of Western Samoan students who matriculated as full-time students at BYU-Hawaii, attending a minimum of one semester during the school years 1978-79 to 1983-84. A further purpose of the study was to identify factors related to the failure of Western Samoan students to prepare as teachers, to graduate from BYU-Hawaii, and to return to Western Samoa to teach for the LDS Church Education System (CES).

It was found that the academic experience of Western Samoan students as BYU-Hawaii has not been successful. Academic difficulties faced by students were associated with financial needs, low maturity level, and inadequate preparation of students in high school English, mathematics, and science. Students had high priorities in obtaining teaching degrees and returning to Western Samoa to teach for the CES. However, a student may choose not to accept a teaching position in the CES in Western Samoa because of the low economy of the country.

von Zur-Muehlen, Max. *German Students in Canada: A Statistical Documentation for the 1980's (Working Paper 85-4).* Ottawa, Ontario: Canadian Higher Education Research Network, April, 1986. 15 p.

Williams, P. R. C. *They Came to Train.* London: H.M.S.O., 1985.

A study of responses to their training experience by study fellows coming to Britain under the British Technical Cooperation Training Programme.

Articles

Bey, Arifin. "Studying in Japan and Its Related Problems". *Research in Higher Education (Daigaku Ronshu)* No. 15 (1986): 47-54.

The article discusses the following problems related to studying in Japan: (1) the difficulty of the Japanese language; (2) the lack of academic and social guidance for foreign students; (3) the problem of degree; and (4) the internationalization of the Japanese society.

Despite all these problems, the author is optimistic about Japan's internationalization of her universities and about

Japan's goal of receiving 100,000 foreign students by the end of this century.

Fraser, Stewart. "Overseas Students and Tertiary Education: Notes on the Australian-Malaysian Link". *Overseas Students and Tertiary Education* 27, No. 1 (1984).

In 1982, 57% of all private overseas students in tertiary training came from Malaysia, and nearly all were of Chinese ethnic origin. Malaysian tertiary students in Australia increased by 35% from 3,965 in 1980 to 5,439 in 1982. This article inquires about the place and role private overseas students played in international understanding and cultural exchange, development assistance, education, and trade-interests of government. The Australian-Malaysian education link is briefly reviewed. The Australian Private Overseas Program is described in terms of its priorities given to students from Malaysia, other Asian countries, Middle Eastern countries, and PNG and the South Pacific.

Hicks, Joe E. "Foreign Students and the Internationalization of the Japanese University". *Research in Higher Education (Daigaku Ronshu)* No. 15 (1986): 15-21.

Talks about the various benefits foreign students would provide to Japanese society and about their current condition in Japan at individual, institutional, and national levels.

Argues that at the individual level, foreign students will promote mutual understanding between Japan and their own country; at the institutional level, they will play an important role in scholarly exchange; and at the national level, they will contribute to mitigating various kinds of conflict between the countries. Points out that despite the fact that the majority of foreign students studying in Japan are from Asian countries, little attention has been paid to their cultures or languages, and that there exist many institutional barriers, such as required examinations or little financial support.

Suggests that in order to promote the internationalization of universities, it is necessary to organize regular meetings to talk about the issue among universities, government, and private industries, as well as within and among universities.

Hicks, J. E. "The Guidance of Foreign Students at Japanese Universities -- A Look at the Organizations and Persons Responsible". *Daigaku Ronshu* No. 13 (1984): 203-223.

This article considers the situation of foreign students in Japan in light of Japanese efforts to increase the number of foreign students studying in Japanese universities. It calls for: (1) more experience and expertise concerning foreign students by Japanese educators and administrators; (2) clear definition of responsibility for foreign students; (3) better coordination among institutions dealing with foreign students; (4) better placement; and (5) more research on foreign students.

Hicks, Joe E. "The Role of Foreign Students in Japan's Internationalization: The Ideal and the Real". *Research in Higher Education (Daigaku Ronshu)* No. 15 (1986): 22-27.

The 13,000 foreign students presently studying in Japan can play an important role in Japan's internationalization. Ideally, foreign students can contribute to a mutual growth process at individual, institutional, and national levels. However, the author contends that several very important preconditions have not been fulfilled for Japan to benefit from receiving foreign students: There is still a lack of personal interest in the majority of foreign students; at the institutional level, there exists a lack of support for privately sponsored foreign students; and the role and the profession of foreign student adviser or counselor is still very weak.

Hicks, J. E. "The Situation of Asian Foreign Students in Japan: Can Japanese Universities Handle a 10-Fold Increase?" In *Higher Education Expansion in Asia*. Hiroshima: Research Institute for Higher Education, Hiroshima University, 1985: 141-153.

An analysis of the problems and possibilities of students from Asian countries who study in Japanese universities in view of Japan's desire to increase the number of foreign students in Japan to 100,000 by the end of the century, this paper deals with such key issues as language problems, the high cost of living in Japan, cultural interaction difficulties, and related factors. The article reports on a survey of Asian students in Japan, discussing their responses to questionnaires. The survey found that most students are satisfied with the education they receive in Japan. However, the difficulty in obtaining a Japanese doctorate because of the specific Japanese academic tradition of graduate study is a deterrent. It was further pointed out that holding the Japanese degree did not have a very high prestige in much of Southeast Asia.

Jones, Philip W. "Overseas Students in Australia". In *Australia's International Relations in Education*, ed. P. Jones (Hawthorn, Australia: Australian Council for Educational Research, 1986): 67-87.

Jurgens, Esther B. "A Current Profile of Students from Taiwan". *NAFSA Newsletter* 37 (October, 1985): 27.

Liu, Jiushi. "Far from Home: Arab Medical Students in Beijing". *China Reconstructs* (9, 1981): 40-42.

Morna, Coleen L. "Innocents Abroad". *Africa Report* (January-February, 1988): 56-58.

Between 1970 and 1978, the foreign student intake in the Soviet Union increased by 125.5%, compared to an increase of 82.4% for the United States. Virtually all foreign students in the USSR have scholarships from Soviet sources. Soviet sources indicate that two million Third World students have trained there since the 1950s and that there are currently 53,000 foreign students in the country. This article focuses on life for foreign students in the Soviet Union, featuring comments from African students on cost of living, adjustment problems, and the like. It is pointed out that Soviet citizens have a general suspicion of foreigners and this created problems, as does the difficulty of obtaining consumer goods and the levels of bureaucracy.

Razzano, Alfredo. "The Conditions of ACP (Africans, Caribbean, and Pacific) Students in the Community". *Courier* (January-February, 1984): 59-61.

Ruediger, Stephan. "International Relationships of Higher Education Institutions in the Federal Republic of Germany". *European Journal of Education* 20, No. 2-3 (1985): 301-308.

Weisbrod, J. "Deutsche Studenten im Ausland (German Students Overseas". *Wirtschaft und Statistik* No. 12 (1985): 942-946.

Williams, Lynn. "Overseas Students in the United Kingdom: Some Recent Developments". *Higher Education Quarterly* 41 (Spring, 1987): 107-118.

The attitudes of both government and Britain's higher education institutions towards overseas students have changed over the last few years. Until fairly recently, overseas students were regarded as little more than a fact of life whose presence was largely a reflection of Britain's post-imperial contacts and responsibilities. They occupied a far-from-central position either educationally or politically. Now, however, the overseas student issue is firmly established on the political agenda, and serious attempts are being made to develop coherent national and institutional policies. In this paper, the author casts some light on how this change has come about by outlining the ways in which British policy has evolved since about 1980 and by briefly analyzing recent trends in overseas student enrollment.

27. Specific Institutional Studies

Books

Bartlett, Kim. *International Student Issues at Quebec Universities (Working Paper 85-2)*. Ottawa, Ontario: Canadian Higher Education Research Network, 1985. 56 p.

Cummings, William K. *East-West Center Degree Student Alumni: Report of a Survey*. Honolulu: East-West Center, 1986. 123 p.

Among the findings and recommendations of a survey of 2,000 participants in the academic programs of the East-West Center:

1. The large majority (9 out of 10) had a positive reaction to their experiences at the center;

2. They had an opportunity to gain a deeper understanding of Asian and Pacific cultures and nations;

3. One-fifth of the participants went on to further study;

4. Many respondents felt that the information provided to them by the center prior to their arrival was incomplete and in some instances misleading. A variety of issues, such as reaction to educational content, extracurricular and cultural activities, and career paths after the center program, are also discussed.

Gomez, Louis Salazar. *International Students in California Community Colleges: A Study of Populations, Programs and Possibilities*. Ed.D. Dissertation, University of Southern California, 1987.

The population of international students in public community colleges has been steadily increasing within the past four decades. Yet comparatively little data have been compiled regarding the makeup of this group and how it is being served.

The purpose of this study, therefore, was to develop a comprehensive profile of foreign students in California community colleges and to determine the extent and adequacy of programs and services being provided.

Major findings included: (1) the current percentage of foreign students in the colleges is approximately 1% of their total population; (2) foreign students currently are predominantly male and single, attend full-time, tend to major in business, engineering or natural sciences, and are primarily planning to transfer to four-year schools; (3) a majority of the colleges have international student programs coordinated by a foreign student adviser or director primarily assigned on a part-time basis; (4) while there appears to be a serious lack of administrative support for providing autonomous departments of international student affairs, moderate support is given to the provision of appropriate levels of staffing; and (5) less than half of the colleges currently seek or provide community support such as family housing, student clubs, or social functions for international students.

Articles

de Winter Hebron, Chris. "Third World Postgraduate Students in a European University -- A Case Study from Newcastle upon Tyne". *Higher Education in Europe* 9 (January-March, 1984): 54-62.

Some of the study problems that students from developing countries encounter in the Department of Architecture of Newcastle University are identified, including skills development (use of English, study technique, and understanding and applying appropriate research methodologies), intellectual pattern, different cultural background, and cognitive structure. Outlines an innovative seminar program designed to reduce some of these problems and analyzes its characteristics -- stress on changing students' cultural attitudes to permit the formation of appropriate cognitive structures or heuristics. Sums up effects of the seminar -- students have become more active and creative learners.

Jimmerson, Ronald M., Trail, Thomas F., and Hastay, Lalid. "Academic Needs of Participant Trainees at Washington State University". *Journal of International Student Personnel* 2, No. 3 (1985): 6-10.

Owen, R. "For Soviet Union, Lumumba University Is a Success in Recruiting Students from Third World". *Chronicle of Higher Education* (February 20, 1985): 35-36.

28. Women International Students

Books

Commonwealth Secretariat. *Towards a Policy for Women Overseas Students in the U.K.* London: Commonwealth Secretariat, 1986.

A report of a conference held to discuss the report "It Ain't Half Sexist, Mum: Women As Overseas Students in the U.K.", this document features the discussions of the conference. Issues such as health services, language issues, social integration, and related topics are discussed as they relate to women overseas students.

Goldsmith, Jane and Shawcross, Valerie. *It Ain't Half Sexist, Mum: Women As Overseas Students in the U.K.* London: World University Service and U.K. Council for Overseas Student Affairs, 1985. 35 p.

Using previously unpublished British Council statistics spanning the period of the U.N. Decade for Women and their own original survey material, the authors paint a disturbing picture of disadvantage, not only academic but also social. Women overseas students:

(1) are only a quarter of all overseas students in U.K., even though over 40% of British students are women;

THE BIBLIOGRAPHY

(2) are "ghetto-ized" in low status courses: only 7% of overseas engineering students are women;

(3) are forced by discriminatory immigration legislation to choose between marriage and study in U.K.;

(4) receive less than a quarter of the scholarships.

Twenty-five recommendations for improvement in this situation are put forward as a call to action for researchers, scholarship-awarding agencies, colleges, local education authorities, welfare officers, women's groups, student unions, and government. The authors stress that women overseas students should be recognized as a special category with specific needs and experiences that must be taken into account at local, national and international levels. They must be included as beneficiaries and as participants in the formulation of policy on overseas students.

Namavar, Massomeh Fereshteh. *Sex-Role Orientation of International Female Graduate Students and Its Relationship with Depression and Anxiety.* Ed.D. Dissertation, Indiana University, 1984. 97 p. Order No. DA8507857

Women preparing for professional careers are exposed to competing role expectations that encourage both conforming to traditional norms (marriage, child rearing) and pursuing a non-traditional role (career). These competing expectations are assumed to have negative consequences for women's mental health. Since attending a foreign graduate school is considered non-traditional behavior for women in most societies, international female students who are attending graduate school may experience anxiety or depression due to their deviation from the societal norm. This distress resulting from role conflict is expected to be particularly great for female graduate students from developing countries, where traditional norms are more widely and more strongly held.

The results supported the following hypotheses: (1) international female graduate students hold less traditional beliefs about women's role than they perceive is held by typical

women in their society; (2) females from developing countries
have more traditional beliefs than those from developed
countries; (3) the longer women have been in graduate school the
less traditional their own sex-role orientation, and the greater
the discrepancy between their own beliefs and their perception
of the typical member of their society; (4) women who perceived
the typical member of their society to be more traditional were
more depressed; (5) females held less traditional beliefs than
males. Other predictions were not supported. Theoretical and
methodological explanations for these findings were presented,
and implications for further research and practice were drawn.

Articles

Abdalla, Saleh E. and Gibson, Janice T. "The Relationship of
Exposure to American Culture on the Attitude of Libyan Nationals
Toward the Role of Women in the Workforce". *Contemporary
Educational Psychology* 9 (July, 1984): 294-302.

This study was designed to determine whether Libyan nationals
in the U.S. for more than four years express more "modern"
attitudes toward the role of women in the workforce.
Questionnaire responses from 100 Libyan students indicated no
relationship between length of stay and attitudes.

Al-Qataee, Abdullah. "The Effect of Exposure to Western Cultures
on the Sex-Role Identity of Saudi Arabians". *Contemporary
Educational Psychology* 9 (July, 1984): 303-312.

The purpose of this study was twofold: (1) to investigate
whether, and to what extent, the Bem Sex Role Inventory (BSRI)
can be applied in Saudi Arabia; and (2) to investigate the effect
on BSRI scores of exposure of Saudi Arabians to Western culture.

Durojaiye, S. M . and Donald, G. A. H. "Students, Wives, and
Mothers: Mature Women Overseas Students". *Higher Education
Review* 16 (Summer, 1984): 57-69.

A study of the motivation and problems of adult women foreign students who are wives and mothers while enrolled at the University College at Cardiff, Wales, looks at their family systems, values, roles, support systems, and stresses. It concludes that more institutional recognition of both the strains and dedication of the women students is warranted.

29. Return and Reentry Issues

Books

Al-Mehawes, M. A. *Saudi Arabian Graduate Returnees: Their Adjustment, Stress and Coping to Adapt and Reintegrate into Saudi Arabia.* Ph.D. Dissertation, University of Denver, 1984.

Ardittis, Solon. *The Assisted Return of Qualified Migrants to Their Countries of Origins.* Geneva: International Labor Office, 1985.

Canadian Bureau for International Education. *Returning Home: A Program for Persons Assisting International Students with the Reentry Process.* Ottawa: Canadian Bureau for International Education, 1984.

Dreisbach, Peter Brainerd. *Readjustment and Life Satisfaction of International Students in Agriculture When Returning to a Developing Country.* Ph.D. Dissertation, Texas A & M University, 1985.

Hood, Mary Ann G. and Schieffer, Kevin, eds. *Professional Integration: A Guide for Students from the Developing World.* Washington, D.C.: National Association for Foreign Student Affairs, 1984. 143 p.

The focus of this comprehensive volume is on the re-integration of foreign graduates from the Third World to their countries on their return from study abroad. Issues such as the continuing education of the returned professional, alumni networking, the professional integration of women, and others are considered.

Plans of Foreign Ph.D. Candidates. Postgraduate Plans of U.S. Trained Foreign Students in Science/Engineering. Fact Sheet to the Vice Chairman, Subcommittee on Economic Goals and Intergovernmental Policy, Joint Economic Committee, Congress of the United States. Washington, D.C.: General Accounting Office, 1986. 11 p.

Articles

Armstrong, G. K. "Life After Study Abroad: A Survey of Undergraduate Academic and Career Choices". *Modern Language Journal* No. 1 (1984): 1-6.

Heym, Sally M. "Reentry: The Student View from Japan". *NAFSA Newsletter* 38 (February, 1987): 1, 7-8.

Hossain, Najimul. "Social Determinants of Foreign Students' Length of Stay in U.S. Following Schooling -- Further Empirical Evidence". *International Journal of Contemporary Sociology* 20 (July-October, 1985): 91-99.

As an extension of prior studies of the brain-drain phenomenon, regression analysis is used to explore causal relationships among variables related to foreign students' stay in the U.S. after graduation. Questionnaire data were collected from 456 foreign students at four U.S. universities. Examined as determinants of expected stay were parents at home, minority ethnic status in native country, child upbringing, sex, marital status, legal obligation to return, job waiting, visa status, politics, and lack of openings in field of specialization. Findings obtained are generally congruent with those predicted on the basis of earlier studies using descriptive statistics.

Lee, Motoko Y. and Ray, Melvin C. "Return Intention of Students from Four Developing Countries". *International Review of Education* 33 (1987): 75-85.

The article compares students from Iran, Nigeria, Taiwan, and Venezuela studying at 30 U.S. universities in 1979 with regard to their perceived likelihood of remaining permanently in the U.S. It finds that their return intention differed by the country of origin, by reasons for remaining in the U.S., and by their anticipated satisfaction with the home country situation upon returning. It also finds that within each country group, the students' return intention differed little in terms of selected personal characteristics, but differed significantly in terms of their reasons for remaining in the U.S. It concludes that the reasons chosen reflected the students' perceptions of the politico-economic situation of their country.

Marks, Martha S. "Preparing International Students in the United States for Reentering the Home Country". *Journal of Multicultural Counseling and Development* 15 (July, 1987): 120-128.

Examines the preparatory needs of international students from developing countries in the areas of both cultural and professional adjustments as they reenter their home countries. These needs indicate that steps be taken through seminars or workshops to prepare international students for challenges they may face when they arrive at home. Reentry challenges are discussed in relation to the home culture and cultural readjustments. Preparation for crossing can be a shared responsibility -- by the student, the host institution, and the home country. Two broad categories of concerns in research on reentry are discussed: (1) cultural concerns -- the issue of culture shock and reverse culture shock; (2) professional concerns, which involve coping with technological differences, material needs, and values orientation. Conclusions include: (1) when preparing foreign students for return to the home country, one must consider factors affecting the student's adjustment; (2) it is appropriate to assist students to adopt a positive framework around their experience abroad.

Martin, J. N. "Communication in the Intercultural Reentry: Student Sojourners' Perception of Change in Reentry Relationships". *International Journal of Intercultural Relations* 10, No. 1 (1986): 1-22.

Martin, J. N. "Intercultural Reentry: Conceptualization and Directions for Future Research". *International Journal of Intercultural Relations* 8, No. 2 (1984): 115-134.

Martin, J. N. "Orientation for the Reentry Experience: Conceptual Overview and Implications for Researchers and Practitioners". In *Theoretical Foundations in Cross-Cultural Orientation Training*, ed. R. Paige (Washington, D.C.: University Press of America, 1985).

Raschio, Richard A. "College Students' Perceptions of Reverse Culture Shock and Reentry Adjustments". *Journal of College Student Personnel* 28 (March, 1987): 156-162.

The author examines college students' perceptions of reverse culture shock and reentry adjustments, reviews reentry programs, and offers recommendations for their improvement. The study was designed to identify: (a) personal factors that mitigate an individual's process of reentry; (b) categories of returnee traits and recommendations to be examined using quantitative tools in later studies; and (c) recommendations for the improvement of reentry support programs. Eighteen returning students at the College of Saint Thomas participated in this study in 1985.

Willis, David. "Strangers in Their Own Country -- The Misfit Returnees". *Far Eastern Economic Review* (January 19, 1984): 67-68.

The author describes the pejorative treatment that children who have lived abroad suffer in their own country -- Japan. Two major reasons are analyzed: (1) the traditional Japanese suspicion of anything strange or different; and (2) the unspoken resentment that too much "foreign-ness" will change the alleged purity of the race and the character of national policies. It is pointed out that in the context of an increasingly interdependent world the Japanese may find the path of undifferentiated national character and culture a difficult one to follow.

30. Alumni

Books

Goodwin, Craufurd D. and Nacht, Michael. *Decline and Renewal: Causes and Cures of Decay Among Foreign-Trained Intellectuals and Professionals in the Third World.* New York: Institute of International Education, 1986.

A report of the findings of an extensive study conducted in Mexico, Indonesia, and Turkey during 1984 and 1985, this volume provides a better understanding of the problem of intellectual and professional decay and attempts to assess its seriousness and to propose solutions. The manifestation of such a decay is twofold: the more tangible and often quantifiable features of this decay are declines in the effectiveness of "decayed persons" in performing the functions for which they were trained, and the less tangible but potentially more important features are the qualitative changes, such as the loss of touch with a discipline or profession and the loss of ethic of research. After a brief analysis of the possible causes for such decay, the authors present some of the decay-prevention schemes in the countries under study. In the concluding section, they outline some policy recommendations for the Third World and the developed world. They include: (1) payment of competitive rates of return; (2) rewards for accomplishment; (3) planned refreshment and renewal; (4) nourishment and support of professional and intellectual communities; (5) involvement in national development; (6) pursuit of scholarly comparative advantage; (7) long-term development linkage; and (8) the global audience.

Nuss, Marianne and Welter, Volker. *Deutschland im Urteil Afrikanischer Lehrer: Eine Befragung in Lesotho zu Ausbildungs und Ruckkehrerproblemen von Stipendiaten, die in der Bundesrepublik zum "Technischen Lehrer" ausgebildet wurden (German in the Judgement of African Students).* Saarbrucken, W. Germany: Verlag Breitenbach, 1986.

This volume reports a study of forty former grant recipients of the Federal Republic of Germany in Lesotho. These Lesotho citizens had received scholarships to study technical subjects in West Germany. They were interviewed after their return home concerning their reactions to West Germany, their social situation during their stay in Germany, their problems of reintegration in Lesotho, and their perceptions of Lesotho's development and prospects. A large majority of the students felt that their job situation was problematic once they returned, and a majority stayed in communication with their German sponsors. The students had a high regard for Germany but criticized the lack of contact with Germans.

Sakabibara, Y. *A Study of Japanese Students at the University of Southern California, 1946-1980: Vocational Impact of American Academic Experience on Japanese Students After Returning to Japan.* Unpublished Doctoral Dissertation, University of Southern California, 1984.

Articles

Arum, Atephen. "Connecting with Alumni Abroad". *NAFSA Newsletter* 38 (March, 1987): 15-17.

Wilson, A. H. "Returned Exchange Students: Becoming Mediating Persons". *International Journal of Intercultural Relations* 9, No. 3 (1985): 285-304.

31. Foreign Student Adviser and Personnel

Books

Academic Advising of Graduate Students from Developing Countries. Washington, D.C.: National Association for Foreign Student Affairs, 1986. 23 p.

As part of a series of handbooks designed to assist faculty advisers of foreign students, this volume provides the framework for an effective advising process through practical, useful information. Aspects discussed include planning and selection, communication with the student prior to arrival, initial campus contact with the student, terms of study, nuts-and-bolts of advising (practical training, field research and thesis advising, etc.), job search, post-educational contact, follow-up, and evaluation. A selected bibliography is included.

Althen, Gary. *Handbook of Foreign Student Advising.* Yarmouth, Maine: Intercultural Press, 1983. 208 p.

A comprehensive guide to foreign student advising aimed at the foreign student adviser, this book is an excellent introduction to the complex roles of the foreign student adviser. The book discusses the nature of the foreign student adviser's position in American colleges and universities. It deals with the necessary characteristics of people involved in foreign student advising and with the attitudes and values as well as the professional standards necessary for foreign student advising. It stresses the different types of knowledge that are necessary for those involved in foreign student advisement, including such topics as applied linguistics, immigration rules, community affairs, external agencies, the internal governance of universities, and the like. Intercultural relations are stressed in this book. It is a very useful general guide to the field of foreign student advisement.

Araya, Belainesh. *The Relationship Between Selected Institutional Personal Characteristics and the Beliefs of International Student Advisers on the Relative Importance of Eight Components of their Work.* Ph.D. Dissertation, The American University, 1987.

Dalili, Farid. *The International Student and United States Higher Education: The Development of International Student Services and a Profile of the Contemporary International Student Office.* Ed.D. Dissertation, University of Akron, 1986.

Greisberger, John E. *Academic Advising of Foreign Graduate Students from Developing Nations*. Ph.D. Dissertation, Iowa State University, 1984. 131 p. Order No. DA8423706

The purpose of this study was to assess the needs of faculty advisers at Iowa State University in advising foreign graduate students from developing nations. Through a systematic sample, 600 Iowa State University graduate faculty members were surveyed by means of a mailed questionnaire.

The findings of this study indicated that faculty advisers perceive that they have special needs in terms of advising foreign graduate students. Additionally, in many instances they believe that they need more information about their foreign advisees than they do about United States advisees in order to advise them effectively. Similarly, certain traits, behaviors, and characteristics important in advising United States graduate students are needed to a greater extent when advising a foreign student. Also determined through this research was that faculty advisers desired to have information about the role and function of the foreign student adviser in order to more effectively advise foreign students. Those surveyed indicated that they would find printed information and orientation sessions on advising foreign students useful.

In general, graduate faculty advisers realize that advising foreign students requires special skills and knowledge. They are committed to providing the best academic advice possible by drawing upon their own experiences, attending information meetings on advising foreign students, and working with the foreign student adviser.

Hung, John Shan-Chuan. *The Role of Foreign Graduate Student Advisers As Perceived by Chinese Students from Taiwan, R.O.C. and Their Academic Advisers in Relation to Students' Expressed Education Satisfaction*. Ed.D. Dissertation, Catholic University of America, 1986.

Khabiri, Mohammad. *Problems Involved in the Academic Advisement Process of Foreign Graduate Students at North Texas State University.* Ph.D. Dissertation, North Texas State University, 1985. 160 p. Order No. DA8515728

This study primarily attempts to determine the problems that were perceived by foreign graduate students, American graduate students, and graduate faculty advisers in the academic advisement process. Comparisons were also made between those three groups by separate specifically designed survey instruments.

The major findings are that: (1) foreign graduate students perceived that their advisers were less interested in them than their advisers indicated; (2) foreign graduate students perceived that they were less satisfied with the advisement process than their faculty advisers believed them to be; (3) foreign graduate students perceived that both parties of the advisement process had performed their roles and responsibilities to a lesser degree than was perceived by faculty advisers; and (4) foreign graduate students and faculty advisers believed that their ability to communicate was a problem area. Major conclusions are as follows: (1) Foreign graduate students misunderstand or are not sufficiently aware of the strength of the commitment of the faculty adviser to the advisement process. (2) Foreign graduate students have higher expectations of the advisement process than do faculty advisers; graduate advisers, by virtue of their professional commitment, naturally feel more positive toward the advising process than do graduate students and are reluctant to admit low-level performance. (3) Cultural factors may lead to students' generalized feelings of frustration and ineffectiveness, for which the adviser and the advising process are blamed. (4) Communication is of crucial importance for the success or failure of the advising process.

Mashburn, Robert and Van de Water, Jack, eds. *Academic Advising in Agriculture for Graduate Students from Developing Countries.* Washington, D.C.: National Association for Foreign Student Affairs, 1984. 58 p.

This publication is aimed at faculty advisers and department chairs in the field of agriculture who deal with foreign students. The information provided is useful and practical. It advises departments to communicate with students prior to arrival, to ensure that requirements are made clear, to be aware of cross-cultural communications issues, and the like. It also deals with end-of-study issues such as practical training, reentry problems and maintaining contact with foreign graduates. This is a very valuable handbook that will be useful not only to agriculturalists but also to others in related fields in the sciences.

McKinney, Jeana. *Making Workshops Work*. Washington, D.C.: National Association for Foreign Student Affairs, 1986. 32 p.

Miri-Shaibani, Vida. *Foreign Student Advisers' Perceptions of Problems Related to Institutional Policies for Foreign Students.* Unpublished Ed.D. Dissertation, Auburn University, 1986. 157 p. Order No. DA8609653

This study examines the perceptions of foreign student advisers of problems related to institutional policies and characteristics for foreign students. Through this study two questions were addressed: (1) What do foreign student advisers perceive as the most important problems for foreign students? (2) Are there any relationships between college characteristics/policies and perceived problems?

Univariate analyses of all items in the questionnaire highlighted foreign students' three most important problem areas as perceived by foreign student advisers: finances, use of the English language, and immigration policies. Chi-square tests were used to determine significant differences between characteristics and policies of colleges and the foreign student advisers' perceptions of problems. From 30 characteristic and policy items, only nine variables were significantly related to the perceived problems of the foreign students. Among the variables, college type showed the most significant relationship with perceived problems. Problem items were classified into eight categories. Each category of problems showed at least one significant relationship with identified policies. The findings, however, indicated that foreign student problems are not closely related to institutional policies. Although some recommendations are made for colleges, problems in areas such as finances (the most significant problem in this study) and immigration policies are beyond the reach of educational institutions. These problems may receive better treatment at the national level.

National Association for Foreign Student Affairs. *Principles for the Administration of Sponsored Student Programs.* Washington, D.C.: National Association for Foreign Student Affairs, 1986.

A set of guidelines for the administration of programs for sponsored (funded) foreign students, this four-page document provides recommendations for the sponsoring agency, the student, and the university hosting the student.

Tabdili, Azar A. *An Evaluation of the Effectiveness of Student Services as Perceived by International Students and Foreign Student Advisers.* Unpublished Ed.D. Dissertation, University of San Francisco, 1984. 206 p. Order No. DA8424809

The purpose of this study was to investigate the effectiveness of foreign student advisers' services in meeting the needs of international students in colleges and universities in and near San Francisco, California.

The main questions of the research addressed differences between student and adviser perceptions regarding the frequency of use, importance, and effectiveness of the services provided by the foreign student adviser's office. Subordinate questions pertained to variations in perceptions related to characteristics of students and advisers.

Generally speaking, international students were significantly more negative in most areas examined by the survey. The students perceived their use of the services as significantly less frequent than advisers, and students perceived the services as significantly less effective. There were also significant differences among groups based on demographic characteristics.

Recommendations included ways in which services could be improved with minimal increases in time or cost to the foreign student advisers: by using volunteer services of "veteran" international students to serve as counselors and as intermediaries between the international students and the foreign student adviser offices, and through newsletters and extended orientation programs.

Articles

Quirino, T. R. and Ramagem, S. P. "The Academic Adviser and the Foreign Graduate Student". *International Education* 15 (Fall, 1985): 37-46.

Examines foreign students' advisers as gate-keepers of access to science and technology. Finds that the five greatest and most frequent problems of foreign students are perceived in an uneven way by the advisers -- difficulties with the language are clearly seen; problems with financial support, adaptation, and housing are not clearly perceived; and knowledge of the scientific method is sharply focused. Stresses that foreign students require greater attention from their advisers in aspects such as cultural adaptation and development and utilization of survival strategies in strange social surroundings. Recommends that advisers should be sensitive to the problems that they experience, especially at the personal level.

Spees, Edith C. and Spees, Emil R. "Internationalizing the Campus: Questions and Concerns". In *Guiding the Development of Foreign Students*, ed. K. Pyle (San Francisco, London: Jossey-Bass, Inc., 1986): 5-18.

Explores the problems and issues of developing a worldview on American campuses and integrating foreign students. Answers the question, "How can student-affairs professionals counter the barriers that inhibit foreign students' involvement in campus life and promote healthy interaction among culturally varied students?" Gives a number of interesting scenarios that provide insight into ways to internationalize a campus. Stresses that internationalizing is a process based on attitude, and that a personal commitment from an internationalizer and support from influential persons of the college and the community can create international programs that respond to local need and interest.

Wortham, F. B. "A Group for Teaching Job Interview Skills to International Students". *Journal of College Student Personnel* 27, No. 2 (1986): 179-181.